WORD by WORD

Beginning Workbook

Steven J. Molinsky · Bill Bliss

Contributing Author
Ann Kennedy

Prentice Hall Regents
Englewood Cliffs, New Jersey 07632

Publisher: Tina Carver
Director of Production and Manufacturing: David Riccardi
Editorial Production/Design Manager: Dominick Mosco
Production Supervision and Page Composition: Jan Sivertsen
Production Coordinator: Ray Keating
Cover Designer: Merle Krumper
Interior Design: Kenny Beck and Jan Sivertsen
Illustrations: Richard E. Hill

© 1995 by Prentice Hall Regents
Prentice-Hall, Inc.
A Simon & Schuster Company
Englewood Cliffs, New Jersey 07632

Printed in the United States of America

10   9   8   7   6   5   4   3   2   1

ISBN 0-13-278269-3

Prentice-Hall International (UK) Limited, London
Prentice-Hall of Australia Pty. Limited, Sydney
Prentice-Hall Canada Inc., Toronto
Prentice-Hall Hispanoamericana, S.A., Mexico
Prentice-Hall of India Private Limited, New Delhi
Prentice-Hall of Japan, Inc., Tokyo
Simon & Schuster Asia Pte. Ltd., Singapore
Editora Prentice-Hall do Brasil, Ltda., Rio de Janeiro

CONTENTS

A. WHAT'S THE WORD?

first	family

1. What's your _____first_____ name?
   John.
2. What's your _____ name?
   Thompson.

apartment	social security	phone

3. What's your _____ number?
   565-7937.
4. What's your _____ number?
   450-78-5785.
5. What's your _____ number?
   602.

zip	area

6. What's your _____ code?
   59633.
7. What's your _____ code?
   212.

B. WHAT'S THE ANSWER?

_d_ 1. What's your surname?   a. 365 44th Avenue.
___ 2. What's your first name?   b. W-∧-T-T-E-R-S-O-N.
___ 3. What's your address?   c. Joseph.
___ 4. How do you spell that?   d. Watterson.
___ 5. What's your apartment number? e. Philadelphia.
___ 6. What's your city?   f. 435-68-5684.
___ 7. What's your telephone number? g. 690-6949.
___ 8. What's your social security number? h. 3B.

C. YOUR APPLICATION

Fill in the form with your personal information.

NAME: _____
      LAST   FIRST   MIDDLE

ADDRESS: _____
         NUMBER   STREET   APT. #

         _____
         CITY   STATE   ZIP CODE

1

A. WHICH GROUP?

wife	husband	mother	father	daughter
son	sister	brother	niece	nephew

- _____wife_____
- _____
- _____
- _____
- _____

- _____
- _____
- _____
- _____

B. HIS NAME OR HER NAME?

His	Her

1. What's your sister's name?
   ___Her___ name is Ellen.

2. What's your nephew's name?
   _____ name is Bob.

3. What's your daughter's name?
   _____ name is Carolyn.

4. What's your grandson's name?
   _____ name is David.

5. What's your husband's name?
   _____ name is Steven.

6. What's your wife's name?
   _____ name is Mary.

C. WHO IS WHO?

_e_ 1. My sister's daughter is   a. my nephew.

___ 2. My mother's father is   b. my son.

___ 3. My father's mother is   c. my mother.

___ 4. My brother's son is   d. my grandmother.

___ 5. My grandfather's daughter is e. my niece.

___ 6. My grandson's father is   f. my grandfather.

D. IN OTHER WORDS

Look at page 2 of the Picture Dictionary. Which word means the same?

1. Mom = _____mother_____   3. Grandpa = _____

2. Dad = _____   4. Grandma = _____

A. WHICH GROUP?

Look at page 3 of the Picture Dictionary. Write each word in the correct place in this diagram.

aunt
_____

_____

_____

_____

_____

_____

_____

_____

_____

_____

B. WHICH WORD?

1. She's my ((aunt) uncle).
   What's (her his) name?

2. (She's He's) my son-in-law.
   Where does (she he) live?

3. (He His) name is John.
   Is he your (niece nephew)?

4. Is she your (niece nephew)?
   Yes. (Her His) name is Sally.

5. Is he your (uncle aunt)?
   No. He's my (cousin sister-in-law).

6. Is (he she) your daughter-in-law?
   Yes. Her (husband father) is my son.

C. WHAT'S THE WORD?

1. Is she your aunt?
   Yes. She's my father's _____ sister _____ .

2. Is he your grandfather?
   Yes. He's my mother's _____ .

3. Is she your mother-in-law?
   Yes. She's my husband's _____ .

4. Is he your brother-in-law?
   Yes. He's my husband's _____ .

5. Is he your nephew?
   Yes. He's my sister's _____ .

6. Is she your niece?
   Yes. She's my brother's _____ .

D. AT PAT AND JIM'S WEDDING

Rita and Sam are at Pat and Jim's wedding. Write the correct words to complete the conversation. Then practice the conversation with a friend.

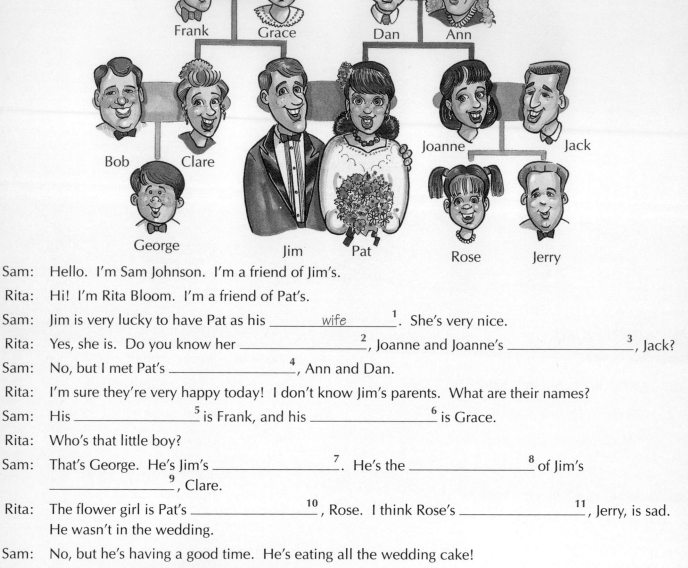

Frank Grace Dan Ann

Bob Clare Joanne Jack

George Jim Pat Rose Jerry

Sam: Hello. I'm Sam Johnson. I'm a friend of Jim's.

Rita: Hi! I'm Rita Bloom. I'm a friend of Pat's.

Sam: Jim is very lucky to have Pat as his _____wife_____[1]. She's very nice.

Rita: Yes, she is. Do you know her _____[2], Joanne and Joanne's _____[3], Jack?

Sam: No, but I met Pat's _____[4], Ann and Dan.

Rita: I'm sure they're very happy today! I don't know Jim's parents. What are their names?

Sam: His _____[5] is Frank, and his _____[6] is Grace.

Rita: Who's that little boy?

Sam: That's George. He's Jim's _____[7]. He's the _____[8] of Jim's _____[9], Clare.

Rita: The flower girl is Pat's _____[10], Rose. I think Rose's _____[11], Jerry, is sad. He wasn't in the wedding.

Sam: No, but he's having a good time. He's eating all the wedding cake!

E. JOURNAL ENTRY

Who is your favorite relative? Why? Tell about him or her.

....

....

....

....

....

....

4

A. USING A COMPASS

Write each word on the correct line.

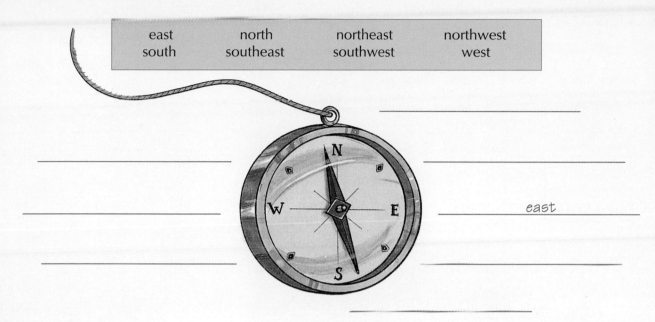

east	north	northeast	northwest
south	southeast	southwest	west

_____

_____   _____

_____   _____ *east*

_____

_____

B. USING THE MAP: *THE U.S.A.*

_c_ 1. Arizona is in the   a. southeast.

___ 2. California is in the   b. east.

___ 3. Maine is in the   c. southwest.

___ 4. Florida is in the   d. west.

___ 5. Washington, D.C. is in the   e. northeast.

___ 6. Washington is in the   f. northwest.

C. WHICH STATES?

Can you name . . .

1. . . . 2 states with *North* in the name? _____North Carolina_____ and _____

2. . . . 2 states with *South* in the name? _____ and _____

3. . . . 1 state with *West* in the name? _____

D. CENTRAL AMERICA AND THE CARIBBEAN

Which country is . . .

1. . . . south of Honduras?   _____Nicaragua_____

2. . . . northwest of Panama?   _____

3. . . . south of Texas?   _____

4. . . . south of Cuba?   _____

5. . . . east of Haiti?   _____

6. . . . west of Belize?   _____

Caribbean Sea

A. WHICH CONTINENT?

Argentina Germany	Austria France	Brazil Japan	Chile Korea	China Nigeria	Egypt Zaire

South America:
- _____Argentina_____
- _____
- _____

Europe:
- _____
- _____
- _____

Asia:
- _____
- _____
- _____

Africa:
- _____
- _____
- _____

B. A TRIP AROUND THE WORLD

Indian	Pacific	Atlantic	Arctic	Mediterranean

We're taking a trip around the world . . . by ship! We're leaving from New York. It takes one week to cross the _____Atlantic_____[1] Ocean to get to England. Then we're going south to Portugal. Then we're going through the _____[2] Sea to get to Italy. Then we're going to visit Egypt and go south through the Red Sea, between Egypt and Saudi Arabia. Then we're going to take a long trip through the _____[3] Ocean to Australia. We're then going northeast through the _____[4] Ocean to Hawaii. We don't want to go north to the _____[5] Ocean! It's too cold!

C. JOURNAL ENTRY

What country do you want to visit some day? Why? Where is it?

....

....

....

....

....

....

EVERYDAY ACTIVITIES 1

A. WHAT DO THEY DO?

washes	get	say	takes	shaves	brushes
combs	go	get	have	puts on	makes

Sally and Sam _____*get*_____ [1] up early every day. He _____ [2] a shower, _____ [3], and _____ [4] his hair. They _____ [5] dressed and _____ [6] breakfast. She _____ [7] her teeth, _____ [8] her face, and _____ [9] makeup. He _____ [10] the beds. They _____ [11] good-bye and _____ [12] to work.

B. CROSSWORD: *PICTURES AND WORDS*

ACROSS

2.

4.

DOWN

1.

3.

(crossword grid)
2. C O M B [3]
4.

C. CROSSWORD: *WHAT DO WE DO?*

ACROSS

1. We have . . . .
4. We eat . . . .

DOWN

2. We make the . . . .
3. We take a . . . .

(crossword grid)
1. B R E A K F A S T
4.

D. WHAT'S THE SEQUENCE?

Put these actions in the best order.

```
___  cook dinner
 1   get up
___  make breakfast
___  have lunch
___  get dressed
___  go to bed
```

📼 E. LISTENING: *EVERYDAY SOUNDS*

Listen to the sounds. Write the number next to the activity.

```
___  taking a shower
___  brushing teeth
 1   taking a bath
___  making dinner
___  shaving
```

A. WHICH WORD?

1. She's vacuuming the (cat (floor)).
2. Are you going to wash the (dishes TV)?
3. I'm going to dust the (piano music).
4. He's going to (exercise play) the piano.
5. I'm going to (iron do) now.

6. I'm going to feed the (dog laundry).
7. Are you going to sweep the (floor baby)?
8. I'm listening to the (radio basketball).
9. She's going to watch (the radio TV).
10. Are you cleaning the (laundry house)?

B. MATCHING

_d_ 1. walk the dog
___ 2. wash the dishes
___ 3. sweep the floor
___ 4. feed the dog
___ 5. study
___ 6. play the guitar

a. give the dog something to eat
b. clean plates, cups, and glasses
c. use a broom
d. take a walk with the dog
e. make music
f. get ready for a test

C. WHAT'S THE ACTION?

feed	do	iron	watch	listen to	play	read

___listen to___
- radio
- music

_____
- laundry
- homework

_____
- shirts
- dresses

_____
- television
- basketball game

_____
- cat
- dog
- baby

_____
- books
- newspapers
- textbooks

_____
- basketball
- guitar
- piano

D. LISTENING: *MORE EVERYDAY SOUNDS*

Listen to the sounds. Put the number of each sound next to the correct sentence.

___ He's sweeping the floor.
_1_ He's doing the laundry.
___ He's vacuuming.
___ He's washing the dishes.
___ He's feeding the baby.

___ He's exercising.
___ He's practicing the piano.
___ He's playing the guitar.
___ He's playing basketball.
___ He's listening to the radio.

A. WHERE ARE THE THINGS?

Look at page 10 of the Picture Dictionary. Write the correct word.

1. There's a _g_ _l_ _o_ _b_ _e_ next to the pencil sharpener.
2. There's an _ _ _ _ _ _ _ projector on the bookshelf.
3. There's a _ _ _ _ _ _ next to the flag.
4. There's an _ _ _ _ _ _ _ next to the chalk on the chalk tray.
5. There's a _ _ _ _ _ _ _ _ _ _ _ _ on the girl's desk.
6. There's a _ _ _ _ _ _ next to the calculator on the girl's desk.

B. MATCHING

_f_ 1. chalk   **a.** paper
___ 2. teacher's   **b.** screen
___ 3. graph   **c.** board
___ 4. movie   **d.** projector
___ 5. bulletin   **e.** aide
___ 6. slide   **f.** tray

C. MATCHING: *COMPOUND WORDS*

Draw a line to complete the word. Then write the word on the line.

1. text   speaker   _textbook_
2. loud   tack   _____
3. thumb   shelf   _____
4. book   book   _____

D. HOW DO WE USE THEM?

| a pencil | a thumbtack | a ruler | chalk | a calculator | a bookshelf |

1. We use this to write on the board.   _chalk_
2. We use this to write on paper.   _____
3. We use this to keep books on.   _____
4. We use this to put papers on a bulletin board.   _____
5. We use this to draw straight lines.   _____
6. We use this to add and subtract numbers.   _____

E. CHECK-OFF LIST

What do you have? What does your classroom have? Put a check next to the items.

I have:

- ___ pen
- ___ pencil
- ___ eraser
- ___ notebook
- ___ graph paper
- ___ ruler
- ___ calculator

My classroom has:

- ___ flag
- ___ clock
- ___ board
- ___ chalk
- ___ globe
- ___ eraser
- ___ bulletin board
- ___ P. A. system
- ___ map
- ___ pencil sharpener
- ___ computer
- ___ bookshelf

CLASSROOM ACTIONS

A. THE TEACHER'S INSTRUCTIONS

1. Raise your (seat (hand)).
2. Erase your (mistake   book).
3. Write your (homework   projector).
4. Go over your (test   board).
5. Pass out the (projectors   papers).
6. Lower (the shade   up).
7. Listen to (the answer   your seat).
8. Erase the (question   hand).
9. Study in (groups   lights).
10. Turn on (the page   the light).

B. WHAT'S THE SEQUENCE?

Put these actions in the best order.

___ Correct your mistakes.

___ Write your name.

___ Check your answers.

___ Hand in your test.

_1_ Take out a piece of paper.

___ Answer the questions.

C. WHAT ARE THEY DOING?

Write a sentence about each classroom action.

1.  _She's writing her name._

2. 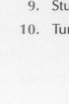 _____

3.  _____

4.  _____

5.  _____

6.  _____

A. LANGUAGES AND COUNTRIES

1. Name 5 countries where the people speak English:

   _____England_____   _____   _____

   _____   _____

2. Name 5 countries where the people speak Spanish:

   _____   _____   _____

   _____   _____

3. Name 3 countries where the people speak Arabic:

   _____   _____   _____

4. Name 2 countries where the people speak Portuguese:

   _____   _____

B. COUNTRY, NATIONALITY, OR LANGUAGE?

1. What's your native language?

   I speak (Saudi (Arabic)).

2. Where are you going on your vacation?

   We're going to (Argentina   Argentine).

3. What country are you from?

   I'm from (France   French).

4. What's your nationality?

   I'm (Taiwan   Taiwanese).

5. Where are you from?

   We're from (Poland   Polish).

6. Do you speak Cambodian?

   No. I speak (Vietnam   Vietnamese).

7. Who is she?

   She's my cousin from (Honduras   Honduran).

8. What's your nationality?

   I'm (Jordanian   Jordan).

9. What language do you speak?

   I speak (Romania   Romanian).

10. What languages do you speak?

    English and (Japan   Japanese).

C. WHAT'S THE WORD?

Our English class has many students from many different countries. Paola is from Italy. She speaks _____Italian_____[1]. Gilberto is Brazilian. He speaks _____[2]. Alicja and Waldek are from _____[3]. They speak Polish. Erdal, from Turkey, speaks _____[4]. Karl is _____[5] and he speaks Latvian. Haija and Sun Hee are _____[6] and speak Korean. Angela is Venezuelan and Adriana is Colombian. They both speak _____[7]. There are many students and many languages, but everyone in our English class has one language that everyone understands: _____[8]!

A. MATCHING

_f_ 1. A private home is

___ 2. There are many apartments in

___ 3. College students often live in

___ 4. A special place for older people is

___ 5. A house on water is

___ 6. A small house in the mountains is

a. a dormitory.

b. a cabin.

c. an apartment building.

d. a houseboat.

e. a nursing home.

f. a single-family house.

B. LISTENING: *CALLING FOR A TAXI*

Listen to the conversation. Write the number next to the correct words.

___ dormitory   ___ townhouse   ___ mobile home   ___ nursing home   _1_ house

C. CROSSWORD

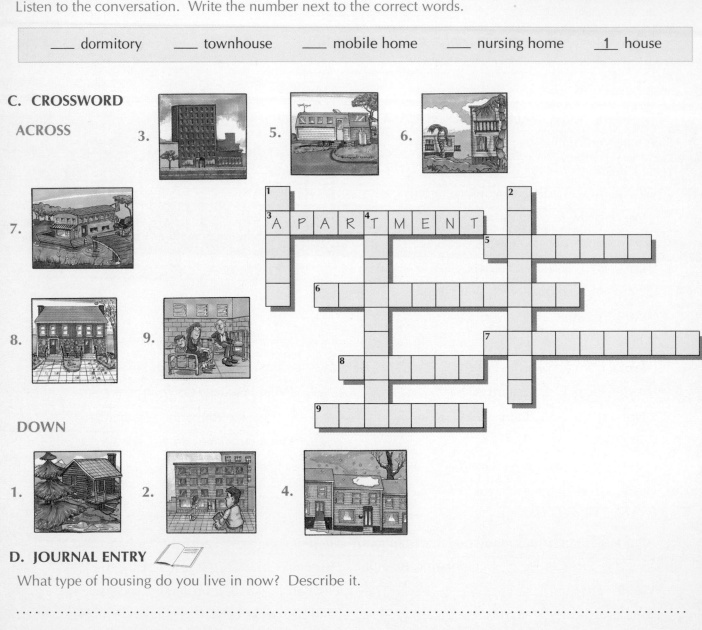

ACROSS

DOWN

D. JOURNAL ENTRY

What type of housing do you live in now? Describe it.

....

....

....

....

A. MAKING LISTS

List 3 things you can sit on:

- _____armchair_____
- _____
- _____

List 4 things you can plug in:

- _____
- _____

- _____
- _____

B. WHERE IS IT?

Look at page 14 of the Picture Dictionary. Write the correct word.

1. There's a _t_ _e_ _l_ _e_ _v_ _i_ _s_ _i_ _o_ _n_ in the entertainment unit.
2. There's a ___ ___ ___ ___ on the end table.
3. There are ___ ___ ___ ___ ___ ___ on the windows.
4. There's a ___ ___ ___ ___ ___ ___ ___ ___ ___ ___ on the bookcase.
5. There's a ___ ___ ___ ___ ___ ___ on the sofa.
6. There's a ___ ___ ___ ___ ___ behind the loveseat.
7. There's a ___ ___ ___ ___ ___ ___ ___ next to the loveseat.

C. ANALOGIES

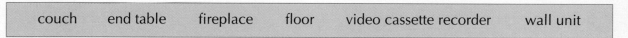

| couch | end table | fireplace | floor | video cassette recorder | wall unit |

1. painting : wall *as* rug : _____floor_____
2. drapes : window *as* screen : _____
3. sofa : loveseat *as* coffee table : _____
4. books : bookcase *as* television : _____
5. drapes : curtains *as* sofa : _____
6. TV : television *as* VCR : _____

D. JOURNAL ENTRY

Imagine you are the cat in the picture on page 14. How do you feel? What are you thinking?

A. MAKING LISTS

List 6 things on the table:

- _____candlestick_____
- _____
- _____
- _____
- _____
- _____

List 4 things on the buffet:

- _____
- _____
- _____
- _____

List 4 things on the serving cart:

- _____
- _____
- _____
- _____

B. MATCHING

_f_ 1. sugar   **a.** pot

___ 2. coffee   **b.** cabinet

___ 3. serving   **c.** shaker

___ 4. salt   **d.** dish

___ 5. butter   **e.** cart

___ 6. china   **f.** bowl

C. MATCHING: *COMPOUND WORDS*

Draw a line to complete the word. Then write the word on the line.

1. tea   stick   _____teapot_____
2. table   pot   _____
3. center   cloth _____
4. candle   piece _____

D. WHICH WORD DOESN'T BELONG?

1. pitcher	(candle)	coffee pot	teapot
2. sugar bowl	china cabinet	buffet	table
3. centerpiece	salt shaker	butter dish	chandelier
4. tablecloth	coffee pot	creamer	sugar bowl
5. table	serving bowl	chair	china cabinet
6. lamp	table	chandelier	candle

E. LISTENING: *WHAT DO THEY NEED?*

Listen to the conversation. Write the number next to the correct words.

___ teapot   ___ coffee pot   _1_ pitcher   ___ butter dish   ___ sugar bowl

A. ON THE TABLE

Look at page 16 of the Picture Dictionary. Write the correct word.

1. The _____wine glass_____ is between the water glass and the cup.
2. The _____ is between the knife and the soup spoon.
3. The _____ is to the left of the teaspoon.
4. The _____ is under the salad fork and the dinner fork.
5. The _____ is on the bread-and-butter plate.
6. The _____ is between the salad fork and the dinner plate.
7. The _____ is under the salad plate.
8. The _____ is to the right of the teaspoon.

B. WHICH WORD?

1. Oops! I dropped my salad (knife   (fork)).
2. This soup (bowl   plate) is very pretty.
3. I'll get a butter (spoon   knife) from the kitchen.
4. I'm sorry I broke the water (napkin   glass).
5. Please get out the cups and (saucers   bowls) so we can serve coffee.
6. Put the (napkin   dinner plate) under the forks.

C. YOUR PLACE SETTING

How do you set a table at home? Draw your place setting below.

Now describe your place setting. Use *on, between, to the right of, to the left of.*

....

....

....

....

....

....

15

THE BEDROOM

A. THINGS FOR THE BEDROOM

Look at page 17 of the Picture Dictionary. Write the correct word.

1. There's a _____headboard_____ at the head of the bed.

2. There's a _____ on the pillow.

3. There's an _____ blanket on the bed.

4. There's an _____ on the nightstand to the left of the bed.

5. There's a _____ above the dresser.

6. There's a _____ on the bureau.

7. There's a _____ on the night table to the right of the bed.

8. There are _____ on the windows.

B. WHICH WORD DOESN'T BELONG?

1. blanket   quilt   bedspread   (cot)

2. blinds   headboard   box spring   footboard

3. pillowcase   clock radio   fitted sheet   flat sheet

4. bunk   mirror   trundle   sofa

5. cot   day bed   twin bed   king-size bed

6. comforter   mirror   quilt   blanket

7. fitted sheet   flat sheet   jewelry box   pillowcase

C. *MAKE THE BED!*

Number these items as they appear on a bed, from top (1) to bottom (6).

____ fitted sheet
____ mattress
_1_ bedspread
____ box spring
____ flat sheet
____ blanket

D. LISTENING: *WHAT IS IT?*

Listen to the conversation about beds. Write the number under the correct picture.

____   ____   ____   ____   _1_

A. WHERE ARE THEY?

Look at page 18 of the Picture Dictionary. Write the correct word.

1. There are two _____ placemats _____ on the kitchen table.

2. The _____ is on the kitchen counter in front of the canisters.

3. There's a _____ on the refrigerator door.

4. The _____ is above the dish rack.

5. The _____ is on the kitchen counter to the left of the can opener.

6. There's a _____ above the stove.

7. The _____ is on the kitchen counter next to the refrigerator.

8. The _____ is below the spice rack.

B. MATCHING

_c_ 1. An ice tray   a. is soap for cleaning dishes.

___ 2. A microwave   b. holds plates, cups, and glasses.

___ 3. A refrigerator   c. makes ice cubes for cold drinks.

___ 4. Dishwashing liquid   d. heats food very quickly.

___ 5. A refrigerator magnet   e. bakes food.

___ 6. A cabinet   f. holds messages to the refrigerator door.

___ 7. An oven   g. keeps food cold.

C. MATCHING: *COMPOUND WORDS*

Draw a line to complete the word. Then write the word on the line.

1. cook   holder   _____ cookbook _____

2. pot   mat   _____

3. place   washer   _____

4. dish   book   _____

D. CROSSWORD

ACROSS

3. trash . . . .
5. cutting . . . .
6. dishwasher . . . .
10. paper towel . . . .

DOWN

1. pot . . . .
2. scouring . . . .
4. microwave . . . .
7. spice . . . .
8. dish . . . .
9. ice . . . .

A. MAKING A LIST

List all of the electrical appliances on page 19 of the Picture Dictionary.

_____   _____   _____

_____   _____   _____

_____   _____   _____

_____   _____

B. WHAT'S THE WORD?

1. We use a _____ coffee _____ _____ grinder _____ to grind coffee.

2. We use a _____ _____ to make popcorn.

3. We use a _____ _____ to open bottles.

4. We use a _____ _____ to open cans.

5. We use an _____ _____ to beat eggs.

6. We use a _____ _____ to peel vegetables.

C. WHICH WORD?

1. It's taking a long time to cut up these onions.
   You need a (cookie cutter (food processor)).

2. I don't like to cut up garlic in little pieces.
   Use this (vegetable peeler   garlic press).

3. Do you want some tea?
   Yes. I'll put the (ladle   kettle) on the stove.

4. This strainer is very small. Do you have something bigger?
   Try this (colander   rolling pin).

5. This soda is hard to open!
   Here. Use this (bottle opener   paring knife).

D. MATCHING: ASSOCIATIONS

_d_ 1. rolling pin   a. cheese

___ 2. grater   b. soup

___ 3. ladle   c. ice cream

___ 4. peeler   d. pies

___ 5. scoop   e. potatoes

A. MATCHING: ASSOCIATIONS

_b_ 1. crib   a. eating
___ 2. intercom   b. sleeping
___ 3. teddy bear   c. playing
___ 4. stroller   d. listening
___ 5. food warmer   e. riding

B. WHICH WORD?

1. Is the baby sleeping?
   Yes. He's in his ((cradle) intercom).

2. I'm looking for the baby's toy.
   Here's her (night light   doll).

3. It's time to eat!
   I'll get the baby's (car seat   high chair).

4. What's that noise?
   It's the baby's (chest   rattle).

5. What will the baby sleep in?
   Her (potty   portable crib).

6. Where should I put this diaper?
   In the (playpen   diaper pail).

7. Where is the baby's stuffed animal?
   Look in the (toy chest   mobile).

8. Let's take a walk!
   Good idea! Put the baby in the
   (booster seat   baby carrier).

C. WHICH WORD DOESN'T BELONG?

1. walker   (mobile)   stroller   carriage
2. crib   doll   rattle   teddy bear
3. playpen   crib   cradle   diaper pail
4. swing   car seat   booster seat   stretch suit
5. stuffed animal   toy chest   crib toy   doll
6. potty   high chair   intercom   baby seat

D. MATCHING

_c_ 1. dressing   a. light
___ 2. teddy   b. chair
___ 3. crib   c. table
___ 4. night   d. pail
___ 5. stretch   e. chest
___ 6. diaper   f. crib
___ 7. toy   g. warmer
___ 8. high   h. bumper
___ 9. portable   i. suit
___ 10. food   j. bear

BABY CARE

A. WHICH WORD?

1. You can wash the baby's hair with this ((shampoo)   food).

2. Give the baby her (diaper pins   vitamins).

3. I have to wash the (formula   teething ring).

4. The baby is crying. Please give him his (pacifier   ointment).

5. She doesn't like milk. She drinks (baby lotion   formula).

6. Please throw those (cloth   disposable) diapers in the trash!

7. I always clean my baby's ears with (cotton swabs   baby wipes).

8. She's a messy eater! Put this (powder   bib) on her before you feed her.

9. He's getting a new tooth. Give him his (teething ring   baby shampoo).

10. We need to buy a new (food   nipple) for this bottle.

B. LISTENING: *WHAT ARE THEY TALKING ABOUT?*

1. (liquid vitamins)	baby wipes	4.	disposable diapers	liquid vitamins
2. diaper pins	teething ring	5.	powder	formula
3. baby wipes	cotton swabs	6.	bottle	pacifier

C. CROSSWORD: *PICTURES TO WORDS*

THE BATHROOM

A. WHERE ARE THEY?

Look at the picture on page 22 of the Picture Dictionary. Write the correct word.

1. The h a m p e r is next to the towel rack.
2. The hair dryer is on the _ _ _ _ _ _.
3. The shower _ _ _ _ _ _ _ is on the shower curtain rod.
4. The _ _ _ _ _ _ is over the sink.
5. A _ _ _ _ _ _ _ _ _ _ _ is in the toothbrush holder.
6. The _ _ _ _ _ _ _ _ is next to the toilet.
7. The _ _ _ is next to the sink.

B. MATCHING

_e_	1. hair	a. holder		___	6. toilet	f. rug
___	2. shower	b. mat		___	7. air	g. rack
___	3. toothbrush	c. towel		___	8. medicine	h. freshener
___	4. hand	d. curtain		___	9. bath	i. paper
___	5. rubber	e. dryer		___	10. towel	j. cabinet

C. WHICH WORD?

1. Clean the tub with this ((sponge)   drain).
2. Put these clothes in the (fan   hamper).
3. Wash your face with (plunger   soap).
4. Put the towel on the (rack   drain).
5. Throw this diaper in the (toilet   wastebasket).
6. How do I turn on the (fan   soap dispenser)?
7. Don't forget to close the (shower curtain   bathtub).
8. Please put the toilet (seat   tank) down.
9. Check your weight with the bathroom (sink   scale).
10. I'm going to take a (bathtub   shower) now.

D. THINGS IN THE BATHROOM

Change one letter to write something you find in the bathroom.

1. van   f a n
2. cut   _ _ _
3. soup   _ _ _ _
4. shell   _ _ _ _ _
5. train   _ _ _ _ _
6. pink   _ _ _ _

A. MATCHING: *ASSOCIATIONS*

_c_ 1. emery board   a. hair

___ 2. comb   b. eyebrows

___ 3. toothbrush   c. fingernails

___ 4. tweezers   d. eyelashes

___ 5. mascara   e. cheeks

___ 6. blush   f. teeth

B. MATCHING: *HOW DO WE USE THEM?*

_c_ 1. dental floss   a. to shine shoes

___ 2. shoe polish   b. to wash hair

___ 3. shampoo   c. to clean between teeth

___ 4. razor   d. to cut fingernails and toenails

___ 5. nail clipper   e. to keep hair neat

___ 6. barrettes   f. for shaving

C. WHICH WORD DOESN'T BELONG?

1. perfume   cologne   (mascara)   deodorant

2. shampoo   shower cap   rinse   conditioner

3. bobby pins   nail polish   hair clips   barrettes

4. mouthwash   hairspray   toothpaste   dental floss

5. tweezers   lipstick   blush   eye shadow

6. emery board   shoe polish   nail polish   nail brush

D. LISTENING: *WHAT ARE THEY TALKING ABOUT?*

Listen to the commercials. What products are they describing? Check the correct answers.

1. ✔ dental floss   4. ___ hair clips   7. ___ blush

   ___ toothbrush   ___ shampoo   ___ brush

2. ___ electric razor   5. ___ lipstick   8. ___ hand lotion

   ___ hairspray   ___ mouthwash   ___ foundation

3. ___ nail polish   6. ___ air freshener   9. ___ deodorant

   ___ shoe polish   ___ hair dryer   ___ styptic pencil

A. WHAT ARE THEY?

Look at page 24 of the Picture Dictionary. Write the correct word.

1. The h a n g e r is over the sink.

2. The _ _ _ _ _ _ _ is between the whisk broom and the broom.

3. The _ _ _ _ _ _ _ _ _ bin is on the floor next to the garbage can.

4. The _ _ _ _ is on the shelf above the ironing board.

5. The _ _ _ _ _ is next to the washing machine.

6. The _ _ _ _ _ _ _ is between the fabric softener and the starch.

7. The _ _ _ _ _ _ is in the pail next to the scrub brush.

8. The _ _ _ _ _ _ _ _ _ _ are on the clothesline.

B. WHICH WORD?

1. There's powder all over the bathroom!
   I'll get the (iron (vacuum)).

2. There's water all over the floor!
   Use this (sponge mop   floor wax).

3. I'll do the laundry.
   Here's the (recycling bin   fabric softener).

4. My clothes are still wet!
   Put them back in the (dryer   dustpan).

5. The dryer isn't working.
   That's okay. Use the (dry mop   clothesline).

6. I can't get these clothes white!
   Did you use (ammonia   bleach)?

7. Did you iron your dress?
   Yes. Now I need a (broom   hanger).

8. Where should I throw this away?
   In the (vacuum cleaner   garbage can) in the corner.

C. MATCHING

_d_ 1. furniture   a. basket

___ 2. fabric   b. sweeper

___ 3. laundry   c. towels

___ 4. washing   d. polish

___ 5. carpet   e. softener

___ 6. dust   f. duster

___ 7. feather   g. cloth

___ 8. paper   h. machine

D. WHICH WORD DOESN'T BELONG?

1.	broom	mop	sweeper	(hanger)
2.	sponge	bin	can	basket
3.	washer	dryer	starch	vacuum
4.	trash can	floor wax	recycling bin	garbage can
5.	cleanser	detergent	bleach	iron
6.	feather duster	laundry bag	whisk broom	dry mop

A. HOME REPAIRS

satellite	doorknob	screens	lamppost	lawn chair
antenna	roof	lawnmower	patio	back

I had a busy weekend. The television didn't work, so I went on the _____ roof _____[1] and checked the TV _____[2] and the _____[3] dish. There was no light on the front walk, so I repaired the _____[4]. The _____[5] door didn't open, so I repaired the _____[6]. I put _____[7] in all the windows. I fixed the _____[8] and then cut the grass with it. After all that work, I wanted to relax, so I repaired the _____[9] and fell asleep in it on the _____[10].

B. MATCHING: *ASSOCIATIONS*

_c_ 1. antenna   a. light   ___ 5. garage   e. fireplace

___ 2. mailbox   b. grass   ___ 6. satellite dish   f. rain

___ 3. lamppost   c. roof   ___ 7. chimney   g. television

___ 4. lawnmower   d. letters   ___ 8. gutter   h. car

C. CROSSWORD

Finish the sentences with one word.

ACROSS

2. Rain leaves the roof through the _____.

4. We cook outside on a _____.

6. We open doors by turning the _____.

7. The TV receives signals through the _____.

8. The postman puts letters in the _____.

DOWN

1. Smoke from the fireplace goes up the _____.

3. The machine that cuts the grass is a _____.

5. Don't knock. Ring the _____.

2 across: D R A I N P I P E

D. JOURNAL ENTRY

Describe a typical home in your country. How is it different from the home on page 25?

....

....

....

THE APARTMENT BUILDING

A. MY APARTMENT BUILDING

elevator	swimming pool	chute	laundry	intercom	doorman
detector	mailboxes	lock	room	peephole	lot

I live in a nice apartment building. In the lobby, there's a _____doorman_____[1] who opens the door. When my friends come, they can call me on the _____[2]. The _____[3] are also in the lobby. To come upstairs to my apartment, you can walk up the stairs, or you can take the _____[4].

There are other nice things about my apartment building. On every floor, there's a garbage _____[5], a _____[6] room, and a storage _____[7]. And outdoors there's a large parking _____[8] and a big _____[9]!

The apartments are safe. Every door has a dead-bolt _____[10] and a _____[11]. In case of fire, every apartment has a smoke _____[12].

I like my apartment very much!

B. MATCHING: COMPOUND WORDS

Draw a line to the correct word. Then write the new word on the line.

1. peep — man   _____peephole_____
2. door — pool   _____
3. mail — hole   _____
4. whirl — box   _____

C. WHICH WORD?

1. When you visit friends at their house, you ring the (buzzer (doorbell)).
2. When you visit friends at their apartment, you enter the lobby and push the (buzzer doorbell).
3. When you park outside, you park in a parking (lot garage).
4. When there's a fire, pull the (smoke detector fire alarm).
5. Throw the trash in the (storage room garbage chute).
6. Leave these boxes in the (storage room garbage chute).
7. When it gets hot in your apartment, turn on the (air conditioner smoke detector).
8. To see someone at your door, look through the (intercom peephole).

D. JOURNAL ENTRY

Describe a typical apartment building in your country. How is it different from the apartment building on page 26?

....
....
....

25

A. REPAIR AND SERVICE PEOPLE

| painter | locksmith | gardener | carpenter | plumber | exterminator |

1. _____locksmith_____
   - doors
   - car doors
   - garage doors
2. _____
   - faucet
   - toilet
   - garbage disposal
3. _____
   - flowers
   - vegetables

4. _____
   - shutters
   - wooden steps
   - bookcase
5. _____
   - ants
   - spiders
   - mice
6. _____
   - walls
   - houses
   - ceilings

B. HELP!

1. I have mice in my kitchen! Do you know a good _____exterminator_____?
2. My drain isn't working. I need a good _____.
3. I have to use the washer. When is the _____ coming?
4. The lights don't work upstairs. I have to call the _____.
5. Call the _____! All our flowers are dying!
6. The fireplace isn't working. Call the _____.
7. When is the _____ going to come? These walls look terrible!
8. My father can do everything around the house. He's a real _____!

C. MATCHING

_e_ 1. house   a. person
___ 2. water   b. bill
___ 3. repair   c. payment
___ 4. chimney   d. fee
___ 5. parking   e. painter
___ 6. mortgage   f. sweep

D. WHAT KIND OF BILLS ARE THESE?

MCI   GE SMITH   Sept. 20, 1999
Acct 212 586 9785

Charges through Sept 10

$4.43	Long Distance Calls
.64	Directory Assistance
16.54	Monthly Service
.58	Federal Tax

$22.19 Total

1. _____ telephone bill _____

City Utilities

Rates for Water/1000 Gal	Consumption thousand gallons	Amounts water
1.36	20	27.20

AMOUNT DUE NOW: $27.20

2. _____

Account number	BILLED FROM	BILLED TO
02204-165573-01-4	06/01	06/30

BALANCE   28.25
Payment   28.25
Monthly Serv 28.25
Amount due   28.25

Cable TV

QUESTIONS: Call customer service at 490-7977

3. _____

Customer Bill

MAR 4 95 Bill for: Please Pay:
456 N. 28th Road $ 62.15
Union City, NJ

METER READINGS		KILOWATT HOUR USAGE	SUMMARY OF CHARGES	
Mar 2	Jan 31		Description	Amount
12650	01990	660	Residential	62.15

FUEL CHARGE	FUEL CHARGE
c/KWHR 1.418	over 800 4.608

Thank you for your last payment—Use Energy Wisely

4. _____

HOME PROTECTION PLAN

DATE	CHARGES	CREDITS	BALANCE
11/19	55.00	0.00	55.00

Explanation: Termite, cockroach, spider extermination

ACCOUNT NO. 21-68495

PLEASE INCLUDE ACCOUNT NUMBER ON ALL CHECKS.

5. _____

U.S. Home Finance Company	PAYMENT #45
San Francisco, CA	
	Due Sep 15
M/M John McKinley	
345 Union Street	
San Francisco, CA 94556	
PAYMENT #45 in the amount of $1,231.50 Due Sept. 15	$1,231.50

6. _____

County Gas Light Company

Meter Reading	CCF of gas used X Therms	
3089 from 3057	32	1.030
	Total Therms	33.0

FOR COMFORT, SAVINGS, AND CONVENIENCE . . .
NATURAL GAS.

AMOUNT DUE NOW: $35.35

7. _____

Suburban Oil Company

Oil Used	52 gals.
Amount due:	$82.45

Want to level off these winter heating bills? Use our budget plan. Call for information.

8. _____

A. HOW ARE THEY USED?

Look at page 28 of the Picture Dictionary. List some of the tools and supplies that are used to . . .

cut | paint | fasten things together
- _____hacksaw_____ | - _____ | - _____
- _____ | - _____ | - _____
- _____ | - _____ | - _____
- _____ | - _____ | - _____

B. WHICH TOOLS?

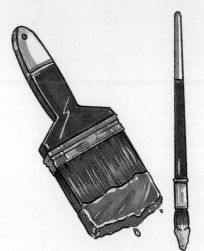

1. Where's the ((hammer)   chisel)? I have to bang in this nail.
2. Give me that (bit   wire) please. I have to drill a hole.
3. I'm going to clean the paintbrushes with the (washer   paint thinner).
4. Before you paint, smooth the wood with the (hacksaw   sandpaper).
5. I'm cutting wood for the fireplace with this (hatchet   vise).
6. Do we have enough (saw   paint) to finish the walls?
7. Careful! That (power saw   bolt) cuts quickly!
8. You can pull that nail out with the (brace   pliers).

C. WHICH WORD DOESN'T BELONG?

1. hammer | wrench | (toolbox) | screwdriver
2. saw | nut | bolt | screw
3. brush | pan | roller | pliers
4. hacksaw | saw | screw | hatchet
5. hammer | hand drill | electric drill | sandpaper
6. wire | wrench | monkey wrench | pliers

D. LISTENING: *WHICH TOOL IS IT?*

Listen to the sounds. Write the number next to the tool you hear.

____ sandpaper   ____ hammer   ____ saw   ____ scraper   _1_ electric drill   ____ power saw

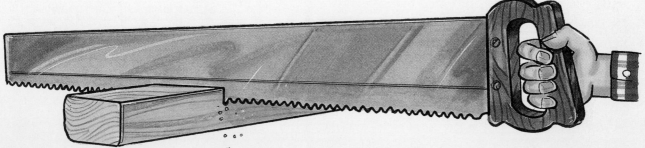

A. WHICH WORD?

1. We have mice! We need a ((mousetrap)   roach killer) right away!

2. We have a problem with the toilet. Where's the (shovel   plunger)?

3. You can measure your height with this (electrical tape   yardstick).

4. I can fix that piece of wood with this (oil   glue).

5. I'm going to plant the (grass seed   vegetable seeds) in the garden.

6. Do you have a (sprinkler   flashlight)? It's dark in here and I can't see a thing!

7. This lamp needs (an extension cord   a garden hose).

8. He's cutting the grass with his new (hoe   lawnmower).

9. They're all over the kitchen sink! Get the (fertilizer   roach killer) now!

10. Hand me that (plunger   fly swatter). I'm going to get that pest!

B. MATCHING: *SENTENCES*

_c_ 1. Where's the hose?

___ 2. Could I borrow your lawnmower?

___ 3. I need the flashlight.

___ 4. Do we have any mousetraps?

___ 5. Where's the tape measure?

___ 6. I need the rake.

___ 7. Could I use your step ladder?

___ 8. Do we have hedge clippers?

a. I need to measure the floor.

b. I saw a mouse in the kitchen.

c. I have to water the grass.

d. I need to cut the grass.

e. I have to paint the ceiling.

f. I have to cut those bushes back.

g. I have to clean up those leaves.

h. I can't see in the dark.

C. MATCHING

_e_ 1. tape

___ 2. electrical

___ 3. bug

___ 4. step

___ 5. work

a. ladder

b. spray

c. gloves

d. tape

e. measure

___ 6. garden

___ 7. gas

___ 8. fly

___ 9. extension

___ 10. hedge

f. swatter

g. cord

h. hose

i. clippers

j. can

D. LISTENING: *WHAT ARE THEY TALKING ABOUT?*

Listen to the conversation. Circle the correct word.

1. hose   (gloves)

2. shovel   trowel

3. tape measure   plunger

4. glue   fuse

5. fly swatter   step ladder

6. hoe   oil

7. fertilizer   nozzle

8. yardstick   insect spray

9. lawnmower   wheelbarrow

A. MATCHING: *CARDINAL AND ORDINAL NUMBERS*

<u>c</u> **1.** four
___ **2.** one
___ **3.** three
___ **4.** two
___ **5.** five
___ **6.** twelve
___ **7.** eight
___ **8.** fourteen

a. fifth
b. twelfth
c. fourth
d. third
e. fourteenth
f. second
g. first
h. eighth

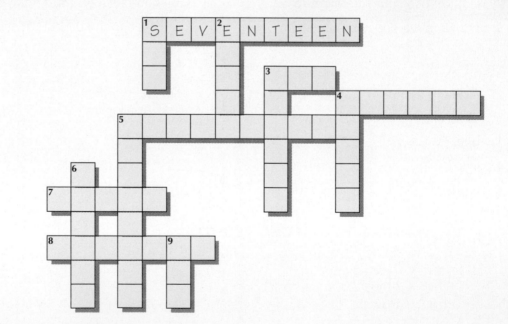

B. WHICH NUMBER?

1. There are ((fifteen) fifteenth) students in the class.

2. We live on the (nine ninth) floor of an apartment building.

3. This is the (three third) time I've been in this country.

4. My daughter is (ten tenth) years old.

5. Today is our (twenty twentieth) wedding anniversary.

6. This is my (twenty-one twenty-first) birthday!

7. We'll have (fifty fiftieth) people at the party.

8. This is the (one first) time I've seen this movie.

C. CROSSWORD: *NUMBERS TO WORDS*

ACROSS

1. 17
3. 10
4. 20
5. 14th
7. 9th
8. 70

DOWN

1. 6
2. 8
3. 12
4. 3rd
5. 40th
6. 90
9. 2

S E V E N T E E N

D. LISTENING: *WHAT'S THE NUMBER?*

Circle the correct number.

1. (nine)   five
2. fifth   first
3. 14   40
4. 7th   11th
5. 20   11
6. 32   42
7. 55   65
8. 13th   30th

A. MATCHING: *WORDS*

<u>c</u> **1.** plus   **a.** multiplication

___ **2.** times   **b.** division

___ **3.** minus   **c.** addition

___ **4.** divided by   **d.** subtraction

B. MATCHING: *NUMBERS AND WORDS*

<u>d</u> **1.** 8 divided by 4 equals 2.   **a.** addition

___ **2.** 4 times 3 equals 12.   **b.** subtraction

___ **3.** 6 plus 2 equals 8.   **c.** multiplication

___ **4.** 9 minus 6 equals 3.   **d.** division

___ **5.** 8 times 2 equals 16.   **e.** $16 - 8 = 8$

___ **6.** 16 divided by 8 is 2.   **f.** $8 \times 2 = 16$

___ **7.** 16 minus 8 equals 8.   **g.** $8 + 8 = 16$

___ **8.** 8 plus 8 is 16.   **h.** $16 \div 8 = 2$

C. MATH SENTENCES

Write the math problems for these sentences.

$3 \times 6 = 18$			

1. *Three times six is eighteen.*   **2.** *Twenty minus six equals fourteen.*   **3.** *Six plus twelve is eighteen.*   **4.** *Twenty divided by two equals ten.*

D. MATCHING: *WORDS AND FRACTIONS*

<u>c</u> **1.** three fourths   **a.** 1/4

___ **2.** two thirds   **b.** 1/2

___ **3.** one quarter   **c.** 3/4

___ **4.** one half   **d.** 1/3

___ **5.** one third   **e.** 2/3

E. WHAT FRACTION IS IT?

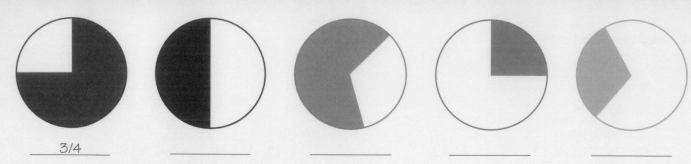

<u> 3/4 </u>   _____   _____   _____   _____

F. LISTENING: *WHAT'S THE FRACTION?*

Listen and write the number under the correct fraction.

1/2	3/4	2/3	1/3	1/4
____	____	____	**1**	____

G. MATCHING: *WORDS AND PERCENTS*

<u> c </u> 1. fifty percent   a. 100%

___ 2. seventy five percent   b. 25%

___ 3. one hundred percent   c. 50%

___ 4. twenty-five percent   d. 60%

___ 5. fifteen percent   e. 75%

___ 6. sixty percent   f. 15%

H. WHAT PERCENT IS IT?

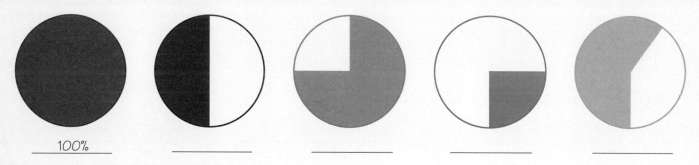

<u> 100% </u>   _____   _____   _____   _____

I. LISTENING: *WHAT'S THE PERCENT?*

Listen and write the number under the correct percent.

25%	75%	50%	100%	60%
____	____	____	**1**	____

J. CLASS PERCENTAGE

1. What percent of your class has brown hair?   . . . .
2. What percent of your class has blue eyes?   . . . .
3. What percent of your class speaks more than two languages?   . . . .
4. What percent of your class speaks more than three languages? . . . .

A. WHAT TIME IS IT?

1. _____4:30_____

2. _____

3. _____

4. _____

5. _____

6. _____

B. MATCHING: *TIME*

Draw a line to the correct time. Then draw a line to the correct words.

1. a quarter to five   5:30   ten to six
2. half past five   5:20   four forty-five
3. five forty   5:50   five thirty
4. five twenty   5:40   twenty to six
5. five fifty   4:45   twenty after five

C. WHEN IS IT?

| midnight | noon | P.M. | A.M. |

1. I usually have breakfast at 7:00 _____.
2. We often eat lunch at _____.
3. Happy New Year! It's exactly _____!
4. Dinner will be served at 7:00 _____.

D. LISTENING: *WHAT'S THE TIME?*

Listen and circle the correct time.

1. (3:00)   3:30
2. 10:05   5:10
3. 1:05   5:01
4. 7:05   5:07
5. 3:45   4:15
6. 8:15   7:45

E. THE TIMES OF YOUR LIFE

What time do you usually . . . .

1. ...get up?   ....
2. ...eat breakfast?   ....
3. ...go to school or work? ....
4. ...have lunch?   ....
5. ...eat dinner?   ....
6. ...go to sleep?   ....

A. TODAY

1. What year is it? .... 3. What day is it? ....
2. What month is it? .... 4. What's today's date? ....

B. USING THE CALENDAR

Look at the calendar on page 33 of the Picture Dictionary. Write your answers.

What day of the week is . . .

1. January 14? _____Thursday_____ 4. January 5? _____
2. January 22? _____ 5. January 11? _____
3. January 2? _____ 6. January 20? _____

C. DATES: *WORDS TO NUMBERS*

Write the date using numbers.

1. September 3, 1949 = _9_/_3_/_49_ 4. February 12, 1995 = ___/___/___
2. January 16, 1970 = ___/___/___ 5. November 10, 1976 = ___/___/___
3. March 26, 1983 = ___/___/___ 6. December 12, 1912 = ___/___/___

D. DATES: *NUMBERS TO WORDS*

Write the date using words.

1. 4/16/78 = _____April 16, 1978_____ 4. 7/20/95 = _____
2. 10/1/96 = _____ 5. 5/25/56 = _____
3. 8/26/80 = _____ 6. 9/3/85 = _____

E. SEQUENCE

Put the months in the correct order.

____ March ____ June ____ November ____ May
____ April ____ February ____ October _1_ January
____ December ____ July ____ August ____ September

F. JOURNAL ENTRY

What are the names and dates of special holidays and celebrations in your country?

A. MAKING A LIST

Look at pages 34-35 in the Picture Dictionary and list 7 places to buy food.

_____bakery_____   _____

_____   _____

_____   _____

   _____

B. WHICH PLACE?

1. I'm getting a haircut today at the ((barber shop) clinic).
2. I'm going to buy bread at the (bank   bakery).
3. Please pick up my coat and my suit at the (dry cleaners   service station).
4. I'll get some medicine at the (health club   pharmacy).
5. Look! There's a sale on sofas and tables at this (furniture store   appliance store)!
6. You can pick up a sandwich and soda at the (concert hall   delicatessen).
7. I'm going to the (service station   convenience store) to get gas and check the oil.
8. Let's get breakfast at the (discount store   donut shop).
9. We bought a beautiful bouquet of roses at the new (computer store   flower shop).
10. We enjoyed the music at the (hospital   concert hall) last night.

C. CROSSWORD: *PICTURES TO WORDS*

ACROSS

2.

3.

4.

5.

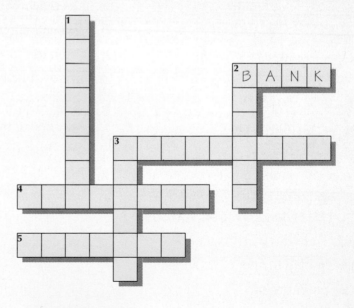

DOWN

1.

2.

3.

A. GOING SHOPPING

We like to shop at the <u>m a l l</u>[1]. We always park in the _ _ _ _ _ _[2]. We buy cassette tapes and CDs at the _ _ _ _ _[3] store. We look at the puppies and kittens at the _ _ _[4] shop. We buy film for our camera at the _ _ _ _ _[5] shop. Our children like to go to the _ _ _[6] store to see all the things to play with. When we get hungry, we eat at the _ _ _ _ _[7] shop or go to a _ _ _ _ _ _ _ _ _ _[8]. We sometimes go to a movie at the movie _ _ _ _ _ _ _ _[9]. We spend a lot of time at the mall!

B. ANALOGIES

travel agency	music store	library	post office	jewelry store	vision center

1. food : supermarket *as* eyeglasses : _____ *vision center* _____
2. toys : toy store *as* jewelry : _____
3. pet shop : zoo *as* book store : _____
4. film : photo shop *as* stamps : _____
5. mothers : maternity shop *as* travelers : _____
6. shoes : shoe store *as* CDs : _____

C. MATCHING: *PLACES AND ACTIONS*

_c_ 1. night club
___ 2. zoo
___ 3. museum
___ 4. mall
___ 5. motel
___ 6. supermarket
___ 7. library
___ 8. laundromat

a. sleep away from home
b. shop at many stores
c. listen to music
d. borrow books
e. wash clothes
f. see special things from the past
g. buy groceries
h. learn about animals

D. LISTENING: *WHERE ARE THEY?*

Listen to the conversation and circle the correct place.

1. (movie theater)   video store
2. train station   motel
3. pet shop   jewelry store
4. travel agency   school
5. shoe store   toy store
6. library   restaurant
7. pizza shop   museum
8. parking garage   ice cream shop

THE CITY

A. WHERE IS IT?

Look at pages 38-39 of the Picture Dictionary and write the answers.

1. There is a taxi in front of the b u s.
2. The subway is under the _ _ _ _ _ _ _.
3. The trash container is on the _ _ _ _ _ _ _ _ _ _.
4. The ice cream truck is on the corner, in front of the _ _ _ _ _ _ _.
5. The police station is next to the _ _ _ _ _ _ _ _ _ _ _.
6. The courthouse is across from the _ _ _ _ _ _ _ _ _ _ _ _ _ _.
7. The newsstand is across from the _ _ _ _ _ _ _ _ _ _ _.
8. The police officer is in the _ _ _ _ _ _ _ _ _ _ _ _.

B. MATCHING: ASSOCIATIONS

d	1. taxi	a.	garbage truck
___	2. newspapers	b.	crosswalk
___	3. pedestrian	c.	newsstand
___	4. fire alarm box	d.	taxi stand
___	5. police station	e.	fire station
___	6. trash container	f.	jail

C. IN THE CITY

meter maid	newsstand	bank	intersection	taxi	crosswalk	street sign	public telephone

1. Pedestrians wait for the green light and then walk in the _____crosswalk_____.
2. The _____ tells the name of the street.
3. It costs twenty-five cents to use a _____.
4. You can buy newspapers at the _____.
5. Use the drive-through window when you go to the _____.
6. Wait at the taxi stand to get a _____.
7. A police officer directs traffic at the _____ of Main Street and Central Avenue.
8. When you don't put enough money in a parking meter, a _____ gives you a ticket.

D. JOURNAL ENTRY

Draw a sketch of an intersection near your home and describe it.

A. WHAT'S THE ANSWER?

Write the correct answer.

1. Is his hair short?

No. It's _____long_____ .

2. Are they good?

No. They're _____ .

3. Is she short?

No. She's _____ .

4. Are his pants tight?

No. They're _____ .

5. Is the water cold?

No. It's _____ .

6. Is she married?

No. She's _____ .

7. Is the street narrow?

No. It's _____ .

8. Are the clothes dry?

No. They're _____ .

9. Are the dishes clean?

No. They're _____ .

B. ANTONYMS

Write the correct opposite.

1. an old man   – a _____young_____ man
2. an old car   – a _____ car
3. a light package – a _____ package
4. a light room   – a _____ room
5. a dull pencil   – a _____ pencil
6. a dull floor   – a _____ floor

7. a short woman   – a _____ woman
8. a short dress   – a _____ dress
9. a hard test   – an _____ test
10. a hard pillow   – a _____ pillow
11. straight hair   – _____ hair
12. a straight road – a _____ road

C. MY CAR

I bought a car yesterday. It isn't (empty (new))[1]. As a matter of fact, it's very (soft old)[2], but it's clean and (messy neat)[3]. It's not (fast curly)[4], but it's very (quiet crooked)[5]. It's not a (fancy thick)[6] car, but it's (pretty ugly)[7]. It's very economical. It's (small narrow)[8], and it won't need a lot of gas. Best of all, the price was (good high)[9]. It was very (inexpensive wealthy)[10] and I like it a lot!

D. CROSSWORD: *OPPOSITES*

Complete the crossword using the *opposites* of the word clues.

ACROSS

4. expensive
6. dry
8. hard
10. crooked
11. cold
12. fancy
13. dull
15. smooth
16. wealthy

DOWN

1. loud
2. slow
3. ugly
5. difficult
7. ugly
9. thick
14. wide

E. JOURNAL ENTRY

Write a word that describes . . . .

1. your street: ....
2. your neighbors: ....
3. your best friend: ....
4. your family: ....
5. your hair: ....
6. your classroom: ....

DESCRIBING PHYSICAL STATES AND EMOTIONS

A. WHICH COLUMN?

happy emotions: *sad* emotions:

_____proud_____   _____

_____   _____

_____   _____

                         _____

proud
annoyed
ecstatic
miserable
disappointed
pleased
frustrated

B. WHICH WORD?

1. I need a sweater. It's ((cold) hot) out!

2. I'm (surprised disgusted)! I got an *A* on my test!

3. I'm (confused thirsty). Let's get something to drink.

4. He feels (sick full). I'm going to take him to the doctor.

5. You look (pretty exhausted). Go to bed early tonight.

C. MATCHING: ASSOCIATIONS

_e_ 1. ill   a. sleep

___ 2. thirsty   b. information

___ 3. confused   c. food

___ 4. hungry   d. drink

___ 5. tired   e. medicine

D. ANALOGIES

unhappy	ecstatic	cold	sick	tired

1. mad : furious *as* happy : _____ecstatic_____

2. scared : afraid *as* ill : _____

3. proud : ashamed *as* hot : _____

4. miserable : sad *as* exhausted : _____

5. angry : mad *as* sad : _____

E. JOURNAL ENTRY

Finish the sentences.

1. When someone interrupts me, I feel . . . .

2. When someone cuts in front of me in line, I feel . . . .

3. When someone bangs into the back of my car, I feel . . . .

4. When a big boy hits a little boy, I feel . . . .

5. When I see . . . . , I feel . . . .

6. When . . . . , I feel . . . .

A. WHICH FRUIT DOESN'T BELONG?

Which fruit . . .

1. isn't a berry?   strawberry   (lime)   blueberry   raspberry
2. isn't a citrus fruit?   coconut   grapefruit   tangerine   lemon
3. isn't a melon?   watermelon   apricot   honeydew   cantaloupe
4. doesn't have a pit?   peach   pineapple   plum   avocado
5. doesn't grow on a tree?   apple   orange   nectarine   strawberry

B. LISTENING: *WHAT FRUIT ARE THEY TALKING ABOUT?*

1. (apples)   apricots   5. watermelon   lemon
2. plums   prunes   6. tangerines   nectarines
3. banana   papaya   7. cherries   cranberries
4. grapes   dates   8. coconut   apricot

C. CROSSWORD: *PICTURES TO WORDS*

ACROSS

3.    5.

6.   8.

9.

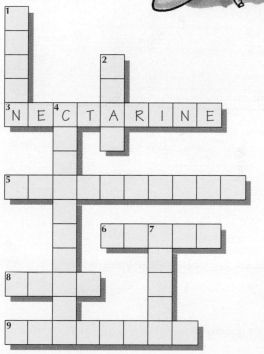

DOWN

1.   2.

4.   7.

A. WHICH GROUP?

| zucchini | lima bean | yam | scallion |

1. string bean   black bean   <u>   lima bean   </u>
2. acorn squash   butternut squash   <u>   </u>
3. potato   sweet potato   <u>   </u>
4. red onion   pearl onion   <u>   </u>

B. MATCHING

<u>b</u> 1. sweet   a. sprouts
___ 2. red   b. potato
___ 3. brussels   c. squash
___ 4. acorn   d. bean
___ 5. string   e. pepper

C. CROSSWORD: *PICTURES TO WORDS*

ACROSS

2.

5.

6.

8.

9.

C A U L I F L O W E R

DOWN

1.

3.

4.

7.

D. JOURNAL ENTRY

People in different countries eat vegetables in different ways. In your country, which vegetables do people eat raw (uncooked)? Which vegetables do people cook before they eat?

Raw: Cooked:

....
....
....
....

A. WHICH GROUP?

canned vegetables	cereal	cheese	eggs
diet soda	milk	noodles	bottled water
rice	soda	soup	tuna fish

Packaged Goods:

_____

_____

_____

Beverages:

_____

_____

_____

Canned Goods:

canned vegetables

_____

_____

Dairy Products:

_____

_____

_____

B. WHICH WORD?

1. I need skim ((milk) punch) for my cereal.
2. We need sour (rice   cream).
3. We also need cottage (fruit   cheese).
4. Tuna (fish   noodle) is good for you.

5. How do you like the pineapple (juice   water)?
6. Finish your fruit (pak   juice).
7. Do we have any juice (fruit   paks)?
8. I'll get some diet (soda   cream).

C. MORE GROUPS

beef	bread	cake	chicken	duck	rolls
salmon	roast	flounder	lamb	shellfish	turkey

Meat:

_____beef_____

_____

_____

Poultry:

_____

_____

_____

Seafood:

_____

_____

_____

Baked Goods:

_____

_____

_____

D. WHERE ARE THEY?

Poultry	Meat	Seafood	Baked Goods	Frozen Foods

1. Drumsticks are in the _____Poultry_____ Section.
2. You can find sausages in the _____ Section.
3. Haddock is in the _____ Section.
4. You'll find rolls in the _____ Section.
5. Ice cream is in the _____ Section.

E. MATCHING: *WHERE ARE THESE FOODS?*

_e_ 1. soup   a. Poultry

___ 2. pork   b. Meat

___ 3. frozen lemonade   c. Beverages

___ 4. chicken   d. Frozen Foods

___ 5. soda   e. Canned Goods

___ 6. cereal   f. Dairy Products

___ 7. bread   g. Seafood

___ 8. eggs   h. Packaged Goods

___ 9. grape juice   i. Baked Goods

___10. flounder   j. Juice

F. WHAT'S THE WORD?

rolls	lemonade	mussels	steak	trout	wings

1. What chicken parts should I get—legs or _____wings_____?

2. What fish do you prefer—salmon or _____?

3. What should I get to drink—orange juice or _____?

4. Would you like shellfish? We have oysters or _____.

5. Beef is on sale today. How about a roast, or a _____?

6. Should we make the sandwiches with pita bread or _____?

G. LISTENING: *WHAT ARE THEY TALKING ABOUT?*

Circle the correct word.

1. cake   (steak)   5. halibut   haddock

2. duck   pork   6. roast   trout

3. ham   lamb   7. oysters   lobsters

4. shrimp   ribs   8. eggs   legs

H. JOURNAL ENTRY

Describe how people shop for food in your country.

....

....

....

....

....

A. WHICH GROUP?

| mozzarella | cocoa | bologna | relish | pretzels | cole slaw |

1. American cheese   provolone   _____mozzarella_____
2. nuts   popcorn   _____
3. potato salad   macaroni salad   _____
4. coffee   tea   _____
5. corned beef   roast beef   _____
6. ketchup   mustard   _____

B. MATCHING

_c_ 1. olive   a. sauce
___ 2. herbal   b. beef
___ 3. corn   c. oil
___ 4. cole   d. chips
___ 5. corned   e. tea
___ 6. soy   f. slaw

C. MATCHING: *ASSOCIATIONS*

_c_ 1. straws   a. weigh
___ 2. soap   b. read
___ 3. tabloid   c. drink
___ 4. cashier   d. clean
___ 5. scale   e. chew
___ 6. gum   f. pay

D. WHICH WORD?

1. I only need a few things. I'll get a shopping (cart   basket).
2. Use paper (towels   bags) to clean up the mess.
3. I forgot to get disposable (diapers   wrap).
4. Household items are in the next (aisle   counter).
5. Do you want a paper or plastic (wrap   bag)?
6. Shoppers can save money when they use (coupons   the cash register).

E. LISTENING: *WHAT SECTION?*

Listen to the conversation and circle the correct section.

1. (Paper Products)   Baking Products
2. Household Items   Checkout Area
3. Baby Products   Dairy Products
4. Coffee and Tea   Snack Foods
5. Baking Products   Jams and Jellies
6. Meat Section   Deli
7. Deli   Condiments
8. Snack Foods   Paper Products

CONTAINERS AND QUANTITIES

A. WHAT'S THE CONTAINER?

bunch	bag	roll	can	box	jar

_____box_____
- cereal
- crackers
- raisins

_____
- toilet paper
- paper towels
- wax paper

_____
- potato chips
- flour
- pretzels

_____
- bananas
- grapes
- carrots

_____
- soup
- tuna fish
- soda

_____
- baby food
- mayonnaise
- jelly

B. WHAT'S THE WORD?

dozen	loaf	ear	box	head	bar	pound	gallon

1. a _____pound_____ of meat
2. a _____ of lettuce
3. a _____ of soap
4. a _____ of milk

5. a _____ of bread
6. a _____ eggs
7. a _____ of crackers
8. an _____ of corn

C. WHICH WORD?

1. I got a ((tub) carton) of margarine.
2. I have two (loaves packs) of gum.
3. Please get a (roll stick) of aluminum foil.
4. Can you get a (half-gallon bunch) of ice cream?
5. We need a (six-pack pound) of butter.
6. Don't forget to buy a (head pack) of lettuce.

☐ D. LISTENING: *WHAT ARE THEY TALKING ABOUT?*

Listen to the conversation and circle the correct words.

1. a six-pack   (two six-packs)
2. a loaf   two loaves
3. a gallon   a half-gallon
4. pack   package

5. bottle   carton
6. a few ears   two ears
7. carton   quart
8. boxes   bunches

A. MATCHING: *ABBREVIATIONS*

_d_ 1. teaspoon   a. Tbsp.
___ 2. tablespoon   b. qt.
___ 3. fluid ounce   c. fl. oz.
___ 4. pint   d. tsp.
___ 5. quart   e. pt.

___ 6. gallon   f. ozs.
___ 7. ounce   g. lbs.
___ 8. pound   h. gal.
___ 9. ounces   i. oz.
___ 10. pounds   j. lb.

B. WHICH IS EQUAL?

_c_ 1. 32 fl. ozs.   a. 1 tablespoon
___ 2. 2 cups   b. 1 gallon
___ 3. 3 tsps.   c. 1 quart
___ 4. 128 fl. ozs.   d. 1 pound
___ 5. 16 ozs.   e. 1 pint

C. WHICH WORD?

1. The recipe says to add 8 ((tablespoons)   quarts) of butter.
2. I need (3/4 lb.   128 fl. ozs.) of ground beef, please.
3. There are two (pounds   cups) of orange juice in this punch.
4. Add a (teaspoon   pound) of salt to the chili.
5. I bought a (pound   gallon) of milk at the supermarket yesterday.
6. The recipe says to put half a (pound   cup) of cream into the mixture.

D. WHAT'S THE NUMBER?

1. 8 fl. ozs. = ___1___ cup   5. 1 gal.   = _____ fl. ozs.
2. 1 pt.   = _____ cups   6. 16 ozs. = _____ lb.
3. 32 fl. ozs. = _____ pints   7. 2 lbs.   = _____ ozs.
4. 2 qts.   = _____ fl. ozs.   8. 6 tsps. = _____ Tbsp.

E. LISTENING

Listen and circle the correct words.

1. two quarts   (two cups)   5. two teaspoons   two tablespoons
2. a cup   a quarter   6. a quarter of a pound   a quart
3. a tablespoon   a teaspoon   7. half a pound   half an ounce
4. half a pint   half a pound   8. pint   quart

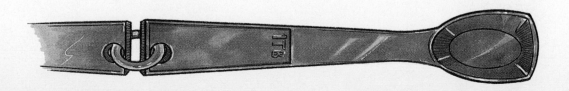

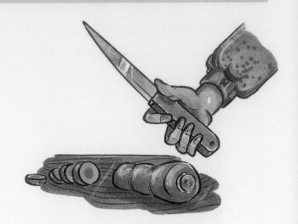

A. MATCHING

_b_ 1. Chop up   a. the turkey.

___ 2. Beat   b. the vegetables.

___ 3. Grate   c. the orange.

___ 4. Peel   d. the lemonade.

___ 5. Pour   e. the cheese.

___ 6. Carve   f. the eggs.

B. HELP IN THE KITCHEN

bake	beat

1. How long should I ___bake___ the chicken?

2. How long should I _____ the eggs?

scrambling	stir-frying

5. I'm _____ the eggs.

6. I'm _____ the vegetables.

pour	slice

3. Please _____ the onion.

4. Please _____ the milk.

boil	barbecue

7. Let's _____ hamburgers.

8. Let's _____ water for tea.

C. SPELLING RULE

> To add -ing: When a verb ends in e, drop the e and add ing.
> slice + ing = slicing

1. He's ___slicing___ bread.

2. She's _____ the turkey.

3. He's _____ eggs.

4. She's _____ cheese.

5. He's _____ potatoes.

6. She's _____ eggs and milk.

A. ORDERING FAST FOOD

<u>c</u> 1. I'd like a slice of

___ 2. I'll have a bowl of

___ 3. I'll have an order of

___ 4. I'd like a bacon, lettuce, and tomato

___ 5. I'll have a small decaf

a. coffee.

b. sandwich.

c. pizza.

d. chili.

e. fried chicken.

B. WHICH WORD DOESN'T BELONG?

1. tea   lemonade   milk   (taco)
2. roll   bun   BLT   bagel
3. tuna fish   roast beef   iced tea   hamburger
4. donut   pumpernickel   whole wheat   rye
5. roast beef   hamburger   corned beef   chicken
6. danish   pita bread   submarine roll white bread

C. LISTENING: *TAKING FAST FOOD ORDERS*

Listen to the order and put a check next to the correct item.

1. ✔ roast beef
   ___ corned beef

2. ___ tuna fish
   ___ biscuit

3. ___ taco
   ___ hot dog

4. ___ danish
   ___ tuna fish

5. ___ chili
   ___ BLT

6. ___ rye bread
   ___ white bread

D. JOURNAL ENTRY

Are any of the fast foods or sandwiches on page 54 of the Picture Dictionary popular in your country?
Which ones? What other foods are popular for a quick meal or snack?

....

....

....

....

....

....

....

....

A. ORDERING

Fill in the blanks, and then practice the conversation with a friend.

| apple pie | veal cutlet | noodles | shrimp cocktail | antipasto |

May I take your order?
　Yes, please. For an appetizer, I'd like the ____shrimp cocktail____[1].
And what kind of salad would you like?
　I'd like the _____[2].
And for the main course?
　I think I'll have the _____[3], please.
What side dish would you like with that?
　I'll have the _____[4].
Would you care for dessert?
　Yes. I'll have _____[5], please.

B. LISTENING: *ORDERING AT A RESTAURANT*

You're a waiter or waitress! Listen to the order and check the correct items.

1.

Appetizers
___ fruit cup/fruit cocktail　___ nachos
___ tomato juice　　　　　　___ chicken wings
___ shrimp cocktail　　　　 ✓ potato skins

Salads
___ tossed salad　　　___ antipasto
___ Greek salad　　　 ___ Caesar salad
___ spinach salad　　 ___ salad bar

Main Courses/Entrees
___ meatloaf　　　___ baked chicken
___ roast beef　　 ___ broiled fish
___ veal cutlet　　 ___ spaghetti

Side Dishes
___ baked potato　　　___ rice
___ mashed potatoes　___ noodles
___ french fries　　　 ___ mixed vegetables

Desserts
___ chocolate cake　___ jello
___ apple pie　　　 ___ pudding
___ ice cream　　　 ___ an ice cream
　　　　　　　　　　　sundae

2.

Appetizers
___ fruit cup/fruit cocktail　___ nachos
___ tomato juice　　　　　　___ chicken wings
___ shrimp cocktail　　　　 ___ potato skins

Salads
___ tossed salad　　　___ antipasto
___ Greek salad　　　 ___ Caesar salad
___ spinach salad　　 ___ salad bar

Main Courses/Entrees
___ meatloaf　　　___ baked chicken
___ roast beef　　 ___ broiled fish
___ veal cutlet　　 ___ spaghetti

Side Dishes
___ baked potato　　　___ rice
___ mashed potatoes　___ noodles
___ french fries　　　 ___ mixed vegetables

Desserts
___ chocolate cake　___ jello
___ apple pie　　　 ___ pudding
___ ice cream　　　 ___ an ice cream
　　　　　　　　　　　sundae

C. ROLE PLAY

You are now the owner of a popular restaurant in your country! Create a menu for your restaurant.

_____'s Restaurant
(Your Name)

Appetizers

_____   _____
_____   _____
_____   _____
_____   _____

Salads

_____   _____
_____   _____
_____   _____

Main Courses/Entrees

_____   _____
_____   _____
_____   _____
_____   _____

Side Dishes

_____   _____
_____   _____
_____   _____
_____   _____

Desserts

_____   _____
_____   _____
_____   _____
_____   _____

Beverages

_____   _____
_____   _____
_____   _____
_____   _____

Now give the menu to some friends who are your restaurant customers, and take down their order.

A. MATCHING: ASSOCIATIONS

_c_ 1. strawberries   a. yellow

___ 2. a lemon   b. purple

___ 3. a carrot   c. red

___ 4. blueberries   d. green

___ 5. lettuce   e. orange

___ 6. eggplant   f. blue

B. WHICH COLOR?

white	black	gold	red	blue	gray	green

1. Look at those _____gray_____ clouds. I think a storm is coming.

2. What a beautiful _____ sky!

3. The grass is so _____!

4. The flag of the United States is _____, _____, and blue.

5. _____ jewelry costs a lot of money.

6. We have an old _____ and _____ TV.

C. QUESTIONNAIRE

Fill in the information about yourself.

1. Color of hair: . . . .

2. Color of eyes: . . . .

3. Favorite color: . . . .

4. Colors on your country's flag: . . . .

D. JOURNAL ENTRY

In the United States, baby girls often wear pink clothing. Baby boys often wear blue. At funerals, people usually wear black or dark clothing. In your country, what colors do people wear in different situations?

. . . .

. . . .

. . . .

. . . .

. . . .

. . . .

. . . .

. . . .

. . . .

A. WHICH WORD?

| sweater | gown | skirt | shirt | suit | jacket |

1. I really like your new short-sleeved _____shirt_____.
2. What a shame! She just ripped her evening _____.
3. I think I'll wear my new cardigan _____ tonight.
4. Where did you get your new sports _____?
5. Wear your three-piece _____ to the wedding.
6. It's too hot for pants. I think I'll wear my new _____.

B. MATCHING: *COMPOUND WORDS*

Draw a line to complete the word. Then write the word on the line.

1. jump   tie   _____jumpsuit_____
2. turtle   neck   _____
3. over   suit   _____
4. neck   alls   _____

C. MAKING CLOTHES

Change the first letter to write a piece of clothing.

1. pie   _t_ _i_ _e_   5. best   _ _ _ _
2. press   _ _ _ _ _ _   6. down   _ _ _ _
3. beans   _ _ _ _ _   7. nights _ _ _ _ _ _ _
4. boat   _ _ _ _ _   8. racket _ _ _ _ _ _ _

D. CROSSWORD: *PICTURES TO WORDS*

ACROSS

1.   4.   5.

6.   7.    8.

DOWN

2.   3.    5.

6.   7.

Crossword grid: 1 Across TURTLENECK

A. WHICH WORD?

1. It's time for bed. Put on your ((pajamas)   work boots).

2. Take off your (long johns   work boots) before you come in the house.

3. I want to play tennis, but I can't find my (flip-flops   sneakers).

4. Those (hiking boots   slippers) look very nice with your nightgown.

5. It's very hot today! I think I'll wear my (high heels   sandals).

6. It's snowing outside! Wear your (boxer shorts   long underwear)
when you go out.

7. You can wear this (robe   panty hose) over your nightgown.

B. WHICH WORD DOESN'T BELONG?

1.	pumps	(underpants)	loafers	sneakers
2.	stockings	sandals	slippers	flip-flops
3.	panties	boxer shorts	boots	underpants
4.	socks	pajamas	tights	stockings
5.	boots	slip	shoes	moccasins
6.	panties	briefs	socks	camisole

C. MATCHING

We wear these. . . .

_g_ 1. . . . at the beach.	a. running shoes
___ 2. . . . at a ball game.	b. sneakers
___ 3. . . . with a bathrobe.	c. high heels
___ 4. . . . climbing a mountain.	d. slippers
___ 5. . . . with a fancy dress.	e. work boots
___ 6. . . . jogging through a park.	f. hiking boots
___ 7. . . . at a construction site.	g. flip-flops

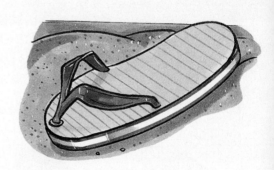

D. LISTENING: *WHAT ARE THEY TALKING ABOUT?*

Listen to the conversation and circle the correct word.

1. athletic supporter   (shorts)

2. high tops   flip-flops

3. slippers   slip

4. pumps   briefs

5. pajamas   panties

6. stockings   socks

7. nightshirt   undershirt

8. shorts   shoes

A. WHICH GROUP?

windbreaker	beret	running shorts	parka	down vest
cap	tennis shorts	rain hat	sweat pants	

jackets   hats   pants

windbreaker _____ _____ _____

_____ _____ _____

_____ _____ _____

B. WHAT DO WE WEAR?

rubbers	shorts	ski jacket	poncho	mittens
tank top	ear muffs	raincoat	sandals	

. . . when it's hot?   . . . when it's raining?   . . . when it's snowing?

_____   _____rubbers_____   _____

_____   _____   _____

_____   _____   _____

C. MATCHING: *WHICH PART OF THE BODY?*

_e_ **1.** ear muffs   **a.** face and head

___ **2.** sweatband   **b.** feet

___ **3.** gloves   **c.** legs

___ **4.** scarf   **d.** forehead

___ **5.** rubbers   **e.** ears

___ **6.** tights   **f.** hands

___ **7.** ski mask   **g.** neck

D. LISTENING: *WHAT ARE THEY TALKING ABOUT?*

Listen to the conversation and circle the correct word.

1. (hat)   cap   **5.** beret   parka

2. poncho   overcoat   **6.** parka   scarf

3. sweatband   sweat pants   **7.** ski mask   ear muffs

4. lycra shorts   trenchcoat   **8.** mittens   tennis shorts

A. WHERE DO WE WEAR THEM?

| ring | necklace | bracelet | beads | belt | watch | wedding band | chain |

neck	finger	wrist	waist
	ring		

B. MATCHING: *HOW DO WE USE THEM?*

_d_ 1. We use these to connect the cuffs of fancy shirts.   **a.** book bag

___ 2. We use this to connect a tie with the shirt.   **b.** belt

___ 3. We use this to keep pants up.   **c.** change purse

___ 4. We keep credit cards and money in this.   **d.** cuff links

___ 5. We carry books in this.   **e.** tie clip

___ 6. We use this to keep keys together.   **f.** umbrella

___ 7. We use this to protect us from the rain.   **g.** key chain

___ 8. We keep coins in this.   **h.** wallet

C. MATCHING: *COMPOUND WORDS*

Draw a line to complete the word. Then write the word on the line.

1. neck   ring   _necklace_

2. pocket   book   _____

3. hand   bag   _____

4. back   case   _____

5. brief   pack   _____

6. ear   lace   _____

D. WHICH WORD DOESN'T BELONG?

1. briefcase   book bag   backpack   (wallet)

2. necklace   key chain   pearls   beads

3. ring   wedding band   key ring   engagement ring

4. bracelet   purse   pocketbook   handbag

5. ring   earrings   bracelet   tote bag

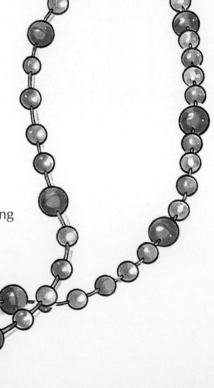

A. WHAT'S THE WORD?

dark	baggy	wide	heavy	low	plain

1. How do you like this fancy tie?

   Actually, I prefer that _____plain_____ one.

2. Shoes with high heels look attractive.

   Yes, but shoes with _____ heels are much more comfortable.

3. These narrow shoes are tight!

   Why don't you try on _____ shoes?

4. Do you think these jeans are too tight?

   No. Actually, I think they're _____.

5. Is it cool enough for a light sweater?

   Actually, I think you should wear a _____ one.

6. Can I wear this light tie with this suit?

   No. A _____ tie looks better.

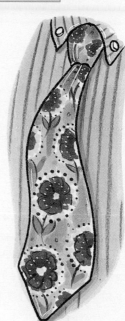

B. WHAT'S THE WORD?

1. This (low (striped)) shirt is half-price.
2. These shoes are too (narrow   baggy).
3. I prefer the (baggy   high) pants.
4. My coat is too (paisley   long).
5. The hiking boots look (light   dark), but they're heavy.
6. This cap is too (short   small) for his head.
7. He prefers to wear a (narrow   tight) tie.
8. The pants are too big and (long   short).

C. LISTENING: *WHAT ARE THEY DESCRIBING?*

Listen to the conversation. Put the number next to the correct description.

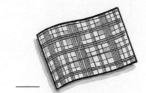

D. WHICH WORD DOESN'T BELONG?

1. dark   light   (tight)
2. large   low   small
3. loose   fancy   baggy
4. long   high   low
5. wide   narrow   short
6. dark   fancy   plain

A. MATCHING: *DEPARTMENTS*

_e_ 1. a tie
___ 2. a necklace
___ 3. a lamp
___ 4. a dress
___ 5. a refrigerator
___ 6. an iron
___ 7. pajamas for a young boy
___ 8. a television

a. Jewelry Counter
b. Furniture
c. Women's Clothing
d. Housewares
e. Men's Clothing
f. Electronics
g. Household Appliances
h. Children's Clothing

B. WHICH WORD?

1. I'm hungry. Let's go to the ((snack bar) Customer Assistance Counter).
2. Where's the Perfume Counter? Let's look at the (water fountain   directory).
3. The car is on the second floor of the (parking lot   elevator).
4. Let's pick up the refrigerator at the (Gift Wrap Counter   customer pickup area).
5. Let's take the (escalator   customer pickup area) up to the third floor.
6. I'm thirsty. Is there a (Customer Service Counter   water fountain) nearby?

C. LISTENING

Listen to the conversation. Write the number next to the correct place.

___ Perfume Counter
_1_ Electronics Department
___ parking garage
___ Children's Clothing Department
___ Furniture Department

___ Jewelry Counter
___ elevator
___ snack bar
___ escalator

D. JOURNAL ENTRY

In your country, where do people buy furniture, clothing, household appliances, and electronic equipment? Do they shop in large department stores or in smaller stores? Describe these places and the items they sell.

....
....
....
....
....
....
....

VIDEO AND AUDIO EQUIPMENT

A. ANOTHER WAY OF SAYING IT

Look at page 63 of the Picture Dictionary. Find another way of saying the same thing.

1. CD = _compact disc_
2. TV = _____
3. VCR = _____
4. Walkman = _____

5. camcorder = _____
6. stereo system = _____
7. portable stereo system = _____
8. tape = _____

B. MATCHING: *ASSOCIATIONS*

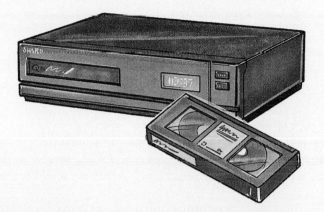

_c_ 1. VCR
___ 2. CD player
___ 3. tape recorder
___ 4. radio
___ 5. turntable

a. record
b. tuner
c. videotape
d. compact disc
e. audio cassette

C. ANALOGIES

| audio cassette | headphones | videotape | Walkman | turntable | VCR |

1. CD : record *as* CD player : _____turntable_____
2. audio cassette : tape deck *as* videotape : _____
3. camcorder : video camera *as* personal cassette player : _____
4. boom box : portable stereo system *as* audio tape : _____
5. tape recorder : audio tape *as* camcorder : _____
6. sound system : speaker *as* Walkman : _____

D. MATCHING: *IDENTIFYING EQUIPMENT*

We use this. . .

_e_ 1. to listen to different stations for news or music.
___ 2. to change the channel on television.
___ 3. to listen to compact discs.
___ 4. to listen to cassettes by ourselves.
___ 5. to wake up to music in the morning.

a. CD player
b. remote control
c. set of headphones
d. clock radio
e. radio

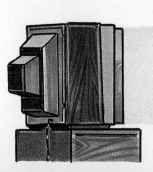

A. MATCHING: *WHAT EQUIPMENT DO YOU NEED?*

We use this. . . .

_e_	1. to take a photograph.	a.	a calculator
___	2. to show slides.	b.	a diskette
___	3. to add, subtract, multiply and divide.	c.	a camera case
___	4. to type.	d.	a slide projector
___	5. to show a movie.	e.	a camera
___	6. to record a telephone message.	f.	an answering machine
___	7. to store information.	g.	a typewriter
___	8. to store a camera.	h.	a movie screen

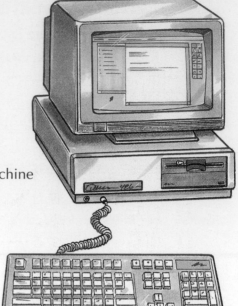

B. MATCHING

_e_	1. fax	a.	drive
___	2. zoom	b.	attachment
___	3. flash	c.	projector
___	4. floppy	d.	telephone
___	5. camera	e.	machine
___	6. disk	f.	lens
___	7. slide	g.	disk
___	8. portable	h.	case

C. LISTENING: *USING A CHECKLIST*

Listen to the conversation. Check the equipment included.

1.
- ✔ monitor
- ___ disk drive
- ___ keyboard
- ___ mouse
- ___ printer
- ___ modem
- ___ software

2.
- ___ monitor
- ___ disk drive
- ___ keyboard
- ___ mouse
- ___ printer
- ___ modem
- ___ software

3.
- ___ camera
- ___ zoom lens
- ___ camera case
- ___ flash attachment
- ___ tripod
- ___ film

A. TOYS

| bicycle | train set | video game system | pail and shovel | jigsaw puzzle | skateboard |

Toys we use inside:

_____

_____

Toys we use outside:

_____ *bicycle* _____

_____

B. MATCHING

e 1. hula   **a.** rope
___ 2. jump   **b.** animal
___ 3. stuffed   **c.** house
___ 4. doll   **d.** ball
___ 5. rubber   **e.** hoop

___ 6. model   **f.** puzzle
___ 7. swing   **g.** figure
___ 8. jigsaw   **h.** set
___ 9. modeling   **i.** kit
___ 10. action   **j.** clay

C. WHAT'S THE WORD?

| coloring book | construction set | doll house | paint set |
| rubber ball | stuffed animal | tricycle | wading pool |

1. You can use your new crayons in your _____ *coloring book* _____.

2. Let's play catch! Throw me that _____.

3. Billy likes to ride his _____ very much.

4. My daughter makes beautiful pictures with her _____.

5. My children built a city with bridges and parks with their _____.

6. It's hot! Let's cool off in the _____.

7. We bought small tables, chairs, rugs, and beds for Patty's _____.

8. My little boy always sleeps with his _____.

D. JOURNAL ENTRY

Write about a special toy you had when you were very young. Why was it special?

....

....

....

....

....

....

....

A. AMERICAN COINS

| penny | nickel | dime | quarter | half dollar | silver dollar |

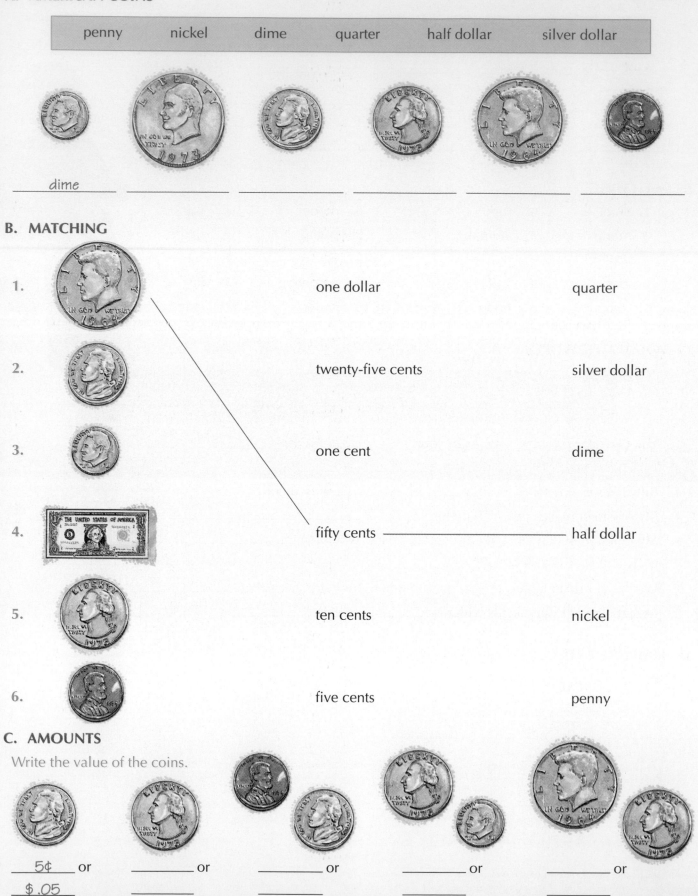

_____dime_____   _____   _____   _____   _____   _____

B. MATCHING

1.

2.

3.

4.

5.

6.

one dollar   quarter

twenty-five cents   silver dollar

one cent   dime

fifty cents ——————————— half dollar

ten cents   nickel

five cents   penny

C. AMOUNTS

Write the value of the coins.

___5¢___ or   _____ or   _____ or   _____ or   _____ or

___$ .05___   _____   _____   _____   _____

D. AMERICAN CURRENCY

Write the value of the currency.

__$10.00__   _____   _____   _____   _____

E. MAKING CHANGE

1. That comes to $16.00.
   Okay. Here's $20.00.
   And your change is ___ $4.00 ___.

2. That will be $.85.
   I have $1.00.
   And your change is _____.

3. And the total is $45.00.
   Here's $50.00.
   Your change is _____.

4. Your total is $8.00.
   I can give you _____.
   Fine. And your change is $2.00.

5. That's $.20.
   I have $.25.
   Okay. And your change is _____.

6. That comes to $99.00.
   Here's _____.
   And here's a dollar back.

F. LISTENING: *HOW MUCH?*

Listen to the conversation. Circle the correct amount.

1. ($10.00)	$.10	5. $5.10	$51.00
2. $25.00	$2.50	6. $23.50	$25.30
3. $1.00	$.01	7. $14.50	$40.60
4. $55.00	$5.50	8. $12.10	$20.10

A. IN THE BANK

traveler's checks	check	monthly statement	teller
checkbook	money order	deposit slip	withdrawal slip

1. Ask the _____ _teller_ _____ for change for $100.

2. We don't accept cash. You can write a _____.

3. I need a _____ for $50.25, please.

4. I can't write a check. I don't have my _____ with me.

5. Don't carry a lot of cash when you go on vacation. It's a good idea to get _____ .

6. The bank will send your _____ in the mail.

7. To put the money in the bank, fill out this _____ .

8. To take money out of the bank, fill out a _____ .

B. MATCHING

_d_ 1. check   a. guard

___ 2. credit   b. order

___ 3. security   c. application

___ 4. money   d. register

___ 5. loan   e. card

___ 6. monthly   f. checks

___ 7. automatic   g. statement

___ 8. traveler's   h. teller

C. WHICH WORD DOESN'T BELONG?

1. teller	security guard	(automatic teller)	bank officer
2. safe deposit box	traveler's checks	check	money order
3. deposit slip	loan application	ATM card	withdrawal slip
4. check register	security guard	monthly statement	bank book
5. check	checkbook	check register	loan application

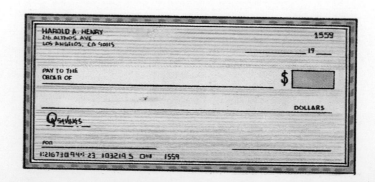

D. WHAT ARE YOU DOING?

Follow the instructions.

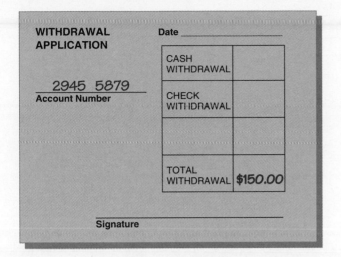

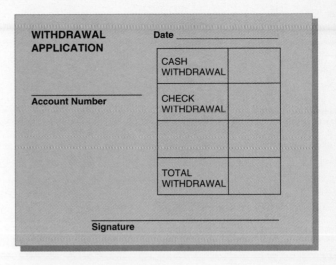

1. Withdraw $150.00.
   Your account number is 2945 5879.

2. Withdraw $250.00.
   Your account number is 1094 3875.

3. Deposit $650.50.
   Your account number is 595 40985.

4. Deposit $450.30.
   Your account number is 4378 349.

5. Write a check for $115.00 to a company or store.

6. Write a check for $36.85 to someone you know.

A. WHICH WORD DOESN'T BELONG?

1. knee (earlobe) calf shin
2. iris cornea pupil nose
3. tongue beard mustache hair
4. forehead nose mouth hip
5. calf knee shin elbow
6. armpit lip teeth tongue

B. MATCHING: *ASSOCIATIONS*

_c_ 1. eyes   **a.** hear
___ 2. ears   **b.** taste
___ 3. nose   **c.** see
___ 4. tongue   **d.** stand
___ 5. teeth   **e.** smell
___ 6. leg   **f.** chew

C. MATCHING: *CLOTHING AND THE BODY*

_e_ 1. tie   **a.** ears
___ 2. belt   **b.** waist
___ 3. hat   **c.** lips
___ 4. stockings   **d.** head
___ 5. lipstick   **e.** neck
___ 6. earrings   **f.** legs

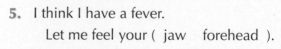

D. WHICH WORD?

1. You look different!
   I'm growing a ((beard) nose).

2. There's a pain in my leg.
   Is it in your (shin skin)?

3. My grandfather fell yesterday.
   Did he hurt his (mustache hip)?

4. What's the matter with your (abdomen chin)?
   I cut it while I was shaving.

5. I think I have a fever.
   Let me feel your (jaw forehead).

6. Can you help me? I can't walk very well.
   When did you break your (arm leg)?

7. I can't bend my (eyelashes knee).
   Call your doctor.

8. I have a sore throat.
   Stick out your (lip tongue) and say "Ah."

E. WHICH WORD DOESN'T BELONG?

1. (bones)   heart   liver   kidneys
2. palm   knuckle   veins   fingernail
3. thumb   toenail   pinky   ring finger
4. ankle   big toe   skin   heel
5. veins   knuckle   heart   arteries
6. pancreas   gallbladder palm   lungs
7. ankle   muscle   wrist   knuckle

F. MATCHING: ASSOCIATIONS

_f_ 1. brain   a. digest food
___ 2. throat   b. point
___ 3. lungs   c. hold
___ 4. stomach   d. breathe
___ 5. heart   e. swallow
___ 6. hand   f. think
___ 7. index finger   g. pump blood

G. MATCHING: CLOTHING AND THE BODY

_e_ 1. watch   a. feet
___ 2. shoes   b. finger
___ 3. gloves   c. neck
___ 4. ring   d. hands
___ 5. scarf   e. wrist

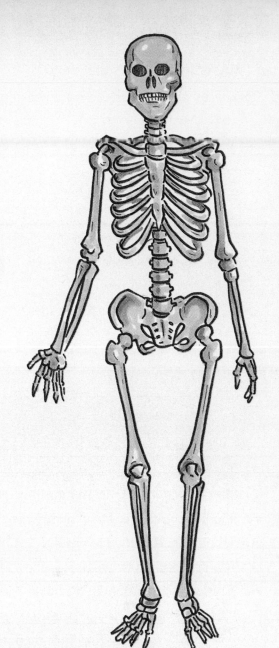

H. WHICH WORD?

1. Charles can't breathe very well.
   Did the doctor check his ((lungs) hip)?

2. Why do you think I'm nervous?
   You're biting your (muscles   fingernails).

3. My sister was in a bad accident!
   Did she break any (toenails   bones)?

4. My mother has chest pains.
   The doctor should check her (skin   heart).

5. I think I ate too much!
   Does your (stomach   spinal cord) hurt?

6. It hurts when I talk!
   I think you have a very sore (throat   thumb).

 I. LISTENING: WHAT IS IT?

Circle the correct word.

1. thumb   (stomach)   5. chin   skin
2. eyelash   tooth   6. nose   bones
3. calf   throat   7. hip   lip
4. back   bladder   8. elbow   little toe

A. MATCHING

Match the sentences that mean the same.

__i__ 1. My head hurts.

___ 2. My throat hurts.

___ 3. I hurt my back.

___ 4. My stomach feels bad.

___ 5. I have a fever.

___ 6. My nose is running.

___ 7. It's hard to talk.

___ 8. My nose is bleeding.

___ 9. My skin is red and it hurts.

___ 10. My ear hurts.

a. I have a backache.

b. I have a temperature.

c. I have a stomachache.

d. I have an earache.

e. I have laryngitis.

f. I have a sore throat.

g. I have a bloody nose.

h. I have a runny nose.

i. I have a headache.

j. I have a sunburn.

B. WHAT'S THE MATTER?

sunburn	stomachache	stiff neck	chills	rash
virus	diarrhea	cavity	backache	sore throat

1. I ate candy all day. Now I have a _____ stomachache _____.

2. Barbara sat in the sun all morning. Now she has a _____.

3. I looked up in the sky all afternoon. Now I have a _____.

4. Donald feels cold. He has the _____.

5. Maria's tooth hurts when she chews food. She has a _____.

6. Bob pulled a muscle in his back. He has a _____.

7. Michael has to go to the bathroom often. He has _____.

8. My wife has a fever, the chills, and a sore throat. She has a _____.

9. Howard is scratching his skin a lot. He has a _____.

10. When Sally swallows, it hurts. She has a _____.

C. JOURNAL ENTRY

Different people and cultures have different ways to stop the hiccups. How do you stop the hiccups? How did you learn this way?

....

....

....

....

....

....

....

D. FEELING TERRIBLE

1. My grandmother fell down.
   Did she ((sprain) burp) her ankle?

2. I feel nauseous.
   Do you think you're going to (bruise   vomit)?

3. I think I have a rash.
   Is it (itchy   bloated)?

4. My husband is sneezing and wheezing.
   He sounds (congested   swollen).

5. I twisted my knee.
   Did you (dislocate   burn) it?

6. My shoes don't fit any more!
   Are your feet (dizzy   swollen)?

7. I'm tired!
   You look (itchy   exhausted)!

8. I feel bloated.
   Try to (scrape   burp).

9. Jane fell down and hurt her knee.
   Is she (cutting   bleeding)?

10. I have a cold. I'm congested.
    Are you (twisting   coughing) a lot?

E. CROSSWORD PUZZLE

ACROSS

1.
2.
4.
6.
8.
9.
10.
11.

DOWN

1.
3.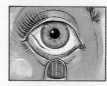
5.
7.

A. MATCHING: *WHAT DO THEY DO?*

a. pediatrician
b. nurse
c. psychiatrist
d. obstetrician
e. gynecologist
f. surgeon
g. cardiologist
h. dentist
i. optometrist
j. oral hygienist

h 1. I take care of people's teeth.

___ 2. I take care of women's health problems.

___ 3. My specialty is children.

___ 4. My specialty is the heart.

___ 5. I help people get the right glasses.

___ 6. I help women have babies.

___ 7. I help the doctor.

___ 8. I help the dentist.

___ 9. I help people solve their problems.

___ 10. My specialty is doing operations.

B. WHAT WILL THEY USE?

Novocaine   X-ray machine   stethoscope   examination table
thermometer   blood pressure gauge   eye chart   scale

1. I'll fill the cavity, but it won't hurt. I'll give you a shot of ___Novocaine___

2. Put this _____ under your tongue.

3. What's your blood pressure? Let's use this _____.

4. Let's take a picture. Please step over here to the _____.

5. I use a _____ to listen to your heart.

6. Please sit down on the _____.

7. I'll check your vision with the _____.

8. How much do you weigh? Please step up on this _____.

C. LISTENING: *WHO'S TALKING?*

Listen to the sentences. Circle the correct answer.

1. (nurse)   psychiatrist   6. cardiologist   pediatrician
2. hygienist   obstetrician   7. gynecologist   cardiologist
3. X-ray technician optometrist   8. lab technician   surgeon
4. dentist   surgeon   9. X-ray technician   optometrist
5. pediatrician   obstetrician   10. psychiatrist   lab technician

MEDICAL TREATMENT AND THE HOSPITAL

A. WHAT DID THE DOCTOR DO?

| sling | cast | diet | exercise | prescription |
| rest | X-ray | crutches | stitches | bandaid |

What did the doctor do. . .

1. . . . for your broken arm?

   He put it in a _____cast_____ and gave me a _____.

2. . . . for your weight problem?

   She gave me a _____ and told me to _____.

3. . . . for your fever?

   She gave me a _____ and told me to _____.

4. . . . for your broken leg?

   He took an _____, put it in a cast, and gave me _____.

5. . . . for the cut on your head?

   She gave me seven _____ and put on a large _____.

B. MATCHING: *WHAT DO THEY DO?*

_d_ **1.** psychiatrists   **a.** analyze blood tests

___ **2.** lab technicians   **b.** do surgery

___ **3.** surgeons   **c.** give injections

___ **4.** X-ray technicians   **d.** give counseling

___ **5.** nurses   **e.** take pictures

C. WHICH WORD?

1. Put on this hospital (bed (gown)).
2. You need to go on a (diet   bandaid).
3. Here's (a prescription   surgery) for your medicine.
4. You can change the position of the bed. Push the bed (control   pan).
5. Take (physical therapy   blood tests) to make your muscles strong.
6. If you can't walk to the bathroom, use the bed (table   pan).
7. The nurse will write the information on the (cast   medical chart).
8. The lab technician put the (I.V.   sling) in my arm.
9. Drink a lot of (gargle   fluids).
10. The doctor gave me a (shot   cast) in my arm.

A. SOLUTIONS

1. My throat hurts.
   Use a throat ((lozenge)   syrup).

2. I'm coughing a lot.
   Take (cough   eye) drops.

3. I'm tired. I don't have any energy.
   Take (vitamins   teaspoons).

4. I have a headache.
   Take two (antacid tablets   aspirins).

5. I have a rash on my back.
   Use this (heating pad   ointment).

6. I have an upset stomach.
   Take (antacid   cold) tablets.

7. I have a stuffy nose.
   Use (decongestant spray   eye drops).

8. My muscles are sore.
   Use this (wheelchair   ointment).

9. I have a rash. It itches a lot.
   Put this (syrup   creme) on it.

10. I have a very bad headache.
    Take (vitamins   aspirin) and rest in bed.

B. WHAT'S THE MEDICINE?

Choose the correct medicine.

1. Take 1 teaspoon every 4 hours.　　　a. aspirin　　　(b.) cough syrup

2. Use two times a day.　　　a. nasal spray　　　b. vitamins

3. Use every night before you go to bed.　　　a. eye drops　　　b. wheelchair

4. Put 2 tablets in a glass of water.　　　a. antacid　　　b. cough drops

5. Use instead of soap.　　　a. ice pack　　　b. creme

6. Take 2 caplets and rest in bed.　　　a. decongestant spray　　　b. aspirin

7. Take 1 every day.　　　a. vitamin　　　b. heating pad

C. LISTENING: *WHAT'S THE DOSAGE?*

Listen to the directions. Circle the correct answer.

1. (3 teaspoons)   6 capsules
2. 1 caplet   1 tablet
3. 2 teaspoons   2 tablespoons
4. 2 capsules   2 caplets

5. 1 pill   1 tablet
6. 1 teaspoon   1 capsule
7. 5 capsules   9 caplets
8. 7 caplets   11 tablets

A. SENDING MAIL

1. I'm going to the post office to mail a ((parcel) postmark).
2. I want to send this package (parcel post   postal clerk), please.
3. A book (of stamps   rate), please.
4. Please mail this (postcard   mailbox) at the post office.
5. I have to mail an air (mail   letter) at the post office.
6. How much is the (postmark   postage)?
7. I'm going to the post office to mail a (letter carrier   letter).
8. I have to send this parcel (mail   post).
9. Write the address on the (zip code   envelope).
10. Buy stamps from the postal clerk or the stamp (machine   postage).
11. The letter carrier forgot his mail (slot   bag).
12. Moving? Don't forget a (selective service registration   change-of-address) form!

B. WHICH WORD DOESN'T BELONG?

1. stamp   address   postmark   (window)
2. mail carrier   postal worker   mail truck   letter carrier
3. air mail   mail bag   registered mail   overnight mail
4. envelope   postcard   aerogramme   mail slot
5. postcard   scale   letter   parcel
6. money order   first class   parcel post   book rate
7. return address   zip code   postage   postal clerk
8. express mail   mailbox   mail truck   mail bag

C. MATCHING

Draw a line to the correct word. Then write the word on the line.

1. registered   rate   _____registered mail_____
2. return   class   _____
3. third   carrier   _____
4. book   address   _____
5. mail   code   _____
6. zip   mail   _____

D. ADDRESSING AN ENVELOPE

You're writing a letter to a friend. Write your friend's address and your return address on the envelope.

A. AT THE LIBRARY

call number	author	shelves	microfilm	magazines	library card
card catalog	title	checkout desk	librarian	assistant	periodicals

To find a book at the library, ask the _____librarian_____[1], or look in the _____[2].
You can look under the name of the _____[3] or the _____[4] of the book.
Then find the _____[5] in the left hand corner of the call card.

Many books are on the _____[6]. There are many newspapers and _____[7]
in the _____[8] section. You can use a special machine to find old
newspapers on _____[9].

To take a book out, give your _____[10] to the
library _____[11] at the _____[12].

B. MATCHING: *LIBRARY HELP*

_e_ 1. I don't know the title or the author.

___ 2. I don't know the meaning of this word.

___ 3. Is there a movie about my subject?

___ 4. I need to look at a map.

___ 5. Where is last week's *New York Times* newspaper?

___ 6. I want to make a copy of this article.

___ 7. Where can I get general information about this person?

a. An atlas is in the reference section.

b. Look in the encyclopedia.

c. The copier is on the second floor.

d. Check in the periodicals section.

e. Look in the card catalog under the subject.

f. Look it up in the dictionary.

g. Go to the media section.

C. READING CALL CARDS

495	Taylor, Sarah F.
	Sports Around the World
215 pg	1993, Sports

648.6	Reynolds, John A.
	The Importance of English
295 pg	1992, Languages

1991, Fiction	
845.66	Field, T.C.
	American Short Stories
335 pg	

1. Who is the author of *The Importance of English*? _____John A. Reynolds_____

2. What is the call number of *Sports Around the World*? _____

3. What is the title of Sarah F. Taylor's book? _____

4. What is the subject of Taylor's book? _____

5. How many pages are in Reynolds' book? _____

6. What year was *American Short Stories* published? _____

7. Which book is about the subject of languages? _____

8. Which book has the call number 845.66? _____

A. AT SCHOOL

1. I'm going to the guidance office to see the (guidance counselor   cafeteria worker).
2. Your teacher is taking a break in the (locker room   teachers' lounge).
3. I'm going to the (cafeteria   chemistry lab) for lunch.
4. Put your books in your (locker   bleachers).
5. I'm going to practice English in the (field   language lab).
6. I'm sick. I'm going to see the (nurse   custodian).
7. Carla likes science. She's often in the (chemistry lab   principal's office).
8. We're going to run around the (coach   track).
9. Let's get a cup of coffee in the (locker room   teachers' lounge).
10. All football players should go to the (language lab   field) for practice.

B. MATCHING: *ASSOCIATIONS*

_f_ 1.	cafeteria worker	a.	classroom
___ 2.	driver's ed instructor	b.	gymnasium
___ 3.	teacher	c.	cafeteria
___ 4.	coach	d.	office
___ 5.	lunchroom monitor	e.	cars, safety
___ 6.	school nurse	f.	food
___ 7.	principal	g.	cleaning
___ 8.	custodian	h.	sickness

C. LISTENING: *WHO ARE THESE STUDENTS GOING TO SEE?*

Circle the correct word.

1. teacher	guidance counselor	5. custodian	counselor
2. custodian	driver's ed instructor	6. lunchroom monitor	assistant principal
3. principal	cafeteria worker	7. custodian	coach
4. lunchroom monitor	school nurse	8. assistant principal	cafeteria worker

SCHOOL SUBJECTS AND EXTRACURRICULAR ACTIVITIES

A. WHERE DO THESE SUBJECTS BELONG?

algebra	biology	calculus	chemistry	English
geometry	physics	Spanish	trigonometry	French

Mathematics:

- _algebra_
- _____
- _____
- _____

Sciences:

- _____
- _____
- _____

Languages:

- _____
- _____
- _____

B. MATCHING: *ASSOCIATIONS*

_e_ 1. grammar, literature

___ 2. countries, mountains, rivers

___ 3. flowers, animals

___ 4. dates, wars, famous people

___ 5. cooking, sewing

___ 6. triangles, squares, circles

___ 7. numbers, addition, subtraction

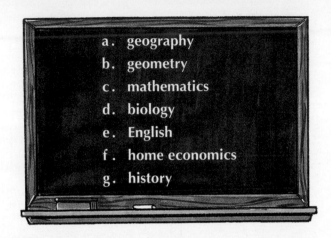

a. geography
b. geometry
c. mathematics
d. biology
e. English
f. home economics
g. history

C. MATCHING: *EXTRACURRICULAR ACTIVITIES*

_g_ 1. I have to practice the violin.

___ 2. I'm acting in a play now.

___ 3. I like to sing.

___ 4. I like to write poetry.

___ 5. I'm president of the class.

___ 6. I like sports.

___ 7. I like to write about school news.

a. He's on the football team.

b. She's in the student government.

c. She works on the literary magazine.

d. She works on the school newspaper.

e. He's in drama.

f. He's in the choir.

g. He's in the orchestra.

D. LISTENING: *WHAT ARE THEY TALKING ABOUT?*

Listen to the sentences and circle the correct words.

1. (choir)   physics
2. art   school newspaper
3. geometry   English
4. driver's education drama
5. Spanish   literary magazine
6. health   football
7. band   typing
8. history   calculus

E. CROSSWORD

ACROSS

1. 3 × 6 = 18
6. All about our bodies
7. Orchestras, bands, and choirs
8. Photographs of all students

DOWN

2. a s d f j k l ;
3. Biology, for example
4. Musicians
5. For actors and actresses

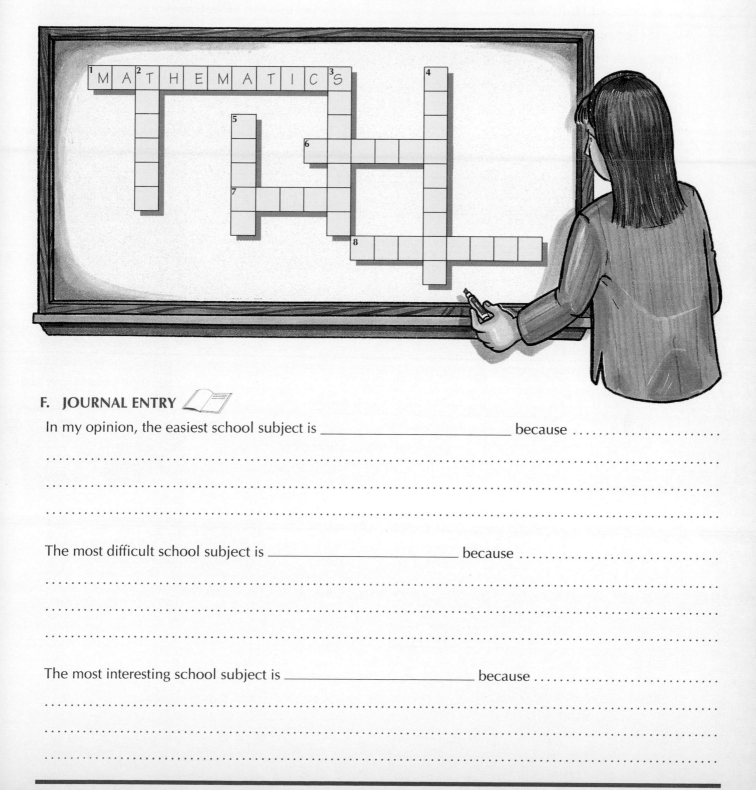

F. JOURNAL ENTRY

In my opinion, the easiest school subject is _____ because . . . .

. . . .

. . . .

. . . .

The most difficult school subject is _____ because . . . .

. . . .

. . . .

. . . .

The most interesting school subject is _____ because . . . .

. . . .

. . . .

. . . .

A. WHAT'S THE WORD?

actress	architect	artist	assembler	baker
bookkeeper	bricklayer	carpenter	cashier	chef

1. I work with money. I use a cash register. I'm a _____cashier_____.
2. Frank is a _____. He makes delicious bread.
3. Rita is a famous Hollywood _____. I saw her in a movie last weekend.
4. Mr. Hanson made the book shelves and fixed our steps. He's a good _____
5. I draw plans for houses and buildings. I'm an _____.
6. Gloria puts parts together in a factory. She's an _____.
7. I draw and paint. I'm studying to be an _____.
8. Mike is a _____. He works on construction sites and builds walls.
9. I keep records of accounts for a business. I'm a _____.
10. My brother-in-law cooks very well. He's a _____.

B. MATCHING: *WHAT DO THEY DO?*

_f_ 1. data processor   a. delivers packages and letters
___ 2. farmer   b. writes articles for newspapers
___ 3. firefighter   c. cleans buildings
___ 4. foreman   d. takes purchases and makes change
___ 5. courier   e. grows vegetables to sell
___ 6. hairdresser   f. designs computer programs
___ 7. butcher   g. cuts and styles hair
___ 8. journalist   h. cuts and prepares meat
___ 9. janitor   i. puts out fires
___ 10. cashier   j. manages a construction crew

C. WHICH GROUP?

accountant	baker	barber	bookkeeper	bricklayer	cashier
chef	courier	custodian	delivery person	hairdresser	housekeeper
		janitor	mason	messenger	

These people cut hair:
- _____
- _____

These people cook:
- _____
- _____

These people clean:
- _____
- _____
- _____

These people deliver:
- _____
- _____
- _____

These people work with numbers and money:
- ____accountant____
- _____
- _____

These people build:
- _____
- _____

D. MATCHING: *COMPOUND WORDS*

Draw a line to complete the word. Then write the word on the line.

1. house   fighter   <u>   housekeeper   </u>
2. book   keeper   _____
3. brick   dresser   _____
4. fire   keeper   _____
5. hair   layer   _____

E. LISTENING: *WHAT'S THE JOB?*

Listen and circle the correct word.

1. (bus driver)   farmer
2. cashier   butcher
3. artist   journalist
4. baker   firefighter
5. barber   fisherman
6. cook   construction worker
7. hairdresser   carpenter
8. bookkeeper   actress

F. CAREER EXPLORATION

Look at pages 80–81 of the Picture Dictionary. Recommend one or more jobs for these people:

I'm good with numbers.

1. <u>   accountant, bookkeeper   </u>

I like to work with my hands.

2. _____

I like to work outside.

3. _____

I'm very creative.

4. _____

I prefer to work alone.

5. _____

I'm a "people person."

6. _____

A. JOBS

| mechanic | newscaster | pharmacist | photographer | real estate agent |
| sanitation worker | police officer | plumber | receptionist | pilot |

1. I like to work on cars. I'm an excellent _____ mechanic _____.
2. Sam can fix the pipes in the kitchen. He's an experienced _____.
3. My sister sells houses. She's a great _____.
4. Jack studied chemistry in college. Now he's a _____.
5. I enjoy people. I work as a _____ in an office.
6. I like to take pictures. I'm a _____ for the city newspaper.
7. Maxine was a journalist. Now she's a _____ on television.
8. I fly airplanes. I'm a _____.
9. Larry collects trash from city neighborhoods. He's a _____.
10. I want to fight crime. Some day I want to be a _____.

B. MATCHING: *WHERE DO THEY WORK?*

_d_ 1. A pharmacist works   a. in a department store.
___ 2. A receptionist works   b. in a lab.
___ 3. A salesperson works   c. in a restaurant.
___ 4. A scientist works   d. in a pharmacy.
___ 5. A teacher works   e. in a garage or service station.
___ 6. A waitress works   f. in an office.
___ 7. A mechanic works   g. in a school.

C. MATCHING: *ASSOCIATIONS*

_b_ 1. waiter   a. languages
___ 2. veterinarian   b. food and drinks
___ 3. translator   c. animals
___ 4. seamstress   d. typewriters and phones
___ 5. secretary   e. dresses and suits
___ 6. photographer   f. cabs
___ 7. pharmacist   g. trash and garbage
___ 8. taxi driver   h. pipes and water
___ 9. sanitation worker   i. medicine
___ 10. plumber   j. camera

D. WHAT'S THE WORD?

paint	paint**er**
interpret	interpret**er**

1. If you paint, you're a _____ painter _____ .

2. If you interpret, you're an _____ .

3. If you garden, you're a _____ .

4. If you report the news, you're a _____ .

5. If you farm, you're a _____ .

6. If you drive a truck, you're a _____ .

7. If you photograph things, you're a _____ .

8. If you wait on people at a restaurant (and you're a man), you're a _____ .

9. If you weld things, you're a _____ .

E. CROSSWORD

ACROSS

1.
4.

5.
7.

8.
9.

DOWN

2.
3.

6.

A. MATCHING: *WHAT DO THEY DO?*

<u>e</u> **1.** Bakers   **a.** draw.

___ **2.** Chefs   **b.** assemble components.

___ **3.** Assemblers   **c.** design buildings.

___ **4.** Artists   **d.** construct things.

___ **5.** Secretaries   **e.** bake.

___ **6.** Architects   **f.** cook.

___ **7.** Carpenters   **g.** file.

___ **8.** Actors   **h.** grow vegetables.

___ **9.** Construction workers   **i.** fly airplanes.

___ **10.** Pilots   **j.** act.

___ **11.** Farmers   **k.** build things.

___ **12.** Security guards   **l.** clean.

___ **13.** Truck drivers   **m.** drive trucks.

___ **14.** Housekeepers   **n.** guard buildings.

B. WHAT DO THEY DO?

1. Painters _____paint_____.

2. Repairpersons _____.

3. Musicians _____.

4. Waiters _____.

5. Seamstresses and tailors _____.

6. Teachers _____.

7. Translators _____.

8. Secretaries _____.

translate
type
sew
paint
serve food
teach
fix things
play an instrument

C. WHAT'S THE WORK ACTIVITY?

bake	draw	assemble	type	grow

_____draw_____	_____	_____	_____	_____
• designs	• letters	• bread	• components	• vegetables
• pictures	• reports	• cookies	• parts	• fruits

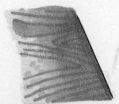
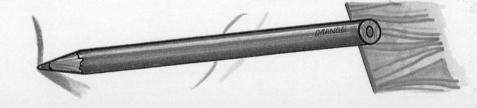

D. MATCHING: *ASSOCIATIONS*

_e_	**1.** sew	**a.**	dishes and clothes
___	**2.** translate	**b.**	lawns
___	**3.** mow	**c.**	food and drinks
___	**4.** serve	**d.**	languages
___	**5.** sing	**e.**	clothing
___	**6.** wash	**f.**	songs

_____

___	**7.** paint	**g.**	broken things
___	**8.** type	**h.**	walls and houses
___	**9.** fly	**i.**	letters and reports
___	**10.** play	**j.**	equipment and machinery
___	**11.** repair	**k.**	music
___	**12.** operate	**l.**	airplanes

E. MATCHING: *WHAT DOES IT MEAN?*

Match the words with the same meaning.

_d_	**1.** assemble components	**a.**	use machinery
___	**2.** mow lawns	**b.**	fix
___	**3.** operate equipment	**c.**	construct
___	**4.** repair	**d.**	put things together
___	**5.** build	**e.**	cut the grass

F. LISTENING: *WHAT DO THEY DO?*

Listen and put a check next to the correct sentence.

1. ✔ I guard buildings.
   ___ I draw things.

2. ___ I deliver food.
   ___ I assemble components.

3. ___ I'm a farmer.
   ___ I'm a veterinarian.

4. ___ I sing.
   ___ I play the piano.

5. ___ I design buildings.
   ___ I construct things.

6. ___ I teach.
   ___ I translate.

7. ___ I type.
   ___ I serve food.

8. ___ I wash dishes.
   ___ I sew.

9. ___ I build things.
   ___ I deliver pizzas.

A. JOE'S DAILY ROUTINE

| coffee machine | workstation | coat closet | waste receptacle |
| mailbox | message board | typist | |

Joe arrives at the office every morning at 8:30. He puts his jacket in the _____coat closet_____[1] and checks his _____[2] for any letters or information. He throws away any *junk* mail in the _____[3]. He always checks the _____[4] for any important messages. Next he goes to the _____[5] to get something to drink. Now he's ready to go to his _____[6] and begin his job as a _____[7].

B. WHICH WORD?

1. Let's go to the ((employee lounge) storage room) and have a cup of coffee.
2. I don't understand. I'm going to ask the (copier   boss).
3. Look in the (supply   file) cabinet for more paper and pens.
4. Someone called for you. I left his name and telephone number in your (file cabinet   mailbox).
5. Ms. Williams is the new (office manager   postage meter).
6. She's in her (office   mailbox).
7. The supplies are in the (waste receptacle   storage room).
8. The workers are at their (employee lounge   workstations).
9. A visitor in the (reception area   storage cabinet) is waiting to see Mrs. Grant.

C. MATCHING: *WHERE IS THIS CONVERSATION TAKING PLACE?*

_e_ 1. "It's out of order again!"   a. at the coffee cart
___ 2. "We'll have 20 people at this meeting."   b. at the postage machine
___ 3. "Good morning. May I help you?"   c. in the conference room
___ 4. "I'm sending it first class."   d. in the reception area
___ 5. "No sugar or cream. I take it black."   e. at the soda machine

D. LISTENING: *WHO IS TALKING?*

Listen and circle the correct answer.

1. (file clerk)   office manager   4. administrative assistant   typist
2. boss   receptionist   5. receptionist   boss
3. typist   file clerk   6. secretary   file clerk

A. WHAT'S THE WORD?

paper shredder	phone system	plastic binding machine
fax machine	calculator	microcassette recorder

1. What's 2.6% of $2,582.80?
   I don't know. Let's use the _____ calculator _____ to find the answer.

2. Can we record this meeting?
   Yes. I brought a _____.

3. Should I send this information in a letter?
   No. They need it right away. Let's use the _____.

4. Can you put all these papers together in a book?
   Yes. We have a _____.

5. There weren't any phone calls this morning.
   Maybe the _____ is broken!

6. This report is confidential. We have to destroy it.
   Don't worry. We have a _____.

B. WHICH WORD?

1. The boss bought a new laser (headset (printer)).
2. Let me show you how to use the word (processor   machine).
3. Do you know how to use the paper (sharpener   shredder)?
4. This is our new phone (machine   system).
5. I weighed the parcel on the postal (scale   machine).
6. I don't have scissors, but you can use the paper (printer   cutter).

C. MATCHING: *ASSOCIATIONS*

_e_ 1. telephone   a. mail

___ 2. paper shredder   b. computer

___ 3. VDT   c. numbers

___ 4. adding machine   d. trash

___ 5. postal scale   e. message

D. LISTENING: *SOUND EFFECTS*

Listen to the sounds of office equipment. Write the number of the sound on the correct line.

___ electric pencil sharpener	___ fax machine	___ adding machine
___ typewriter	_1_ telephone	___ dot-matrix printer

A. WHICH GROUP?

| clerical | highlighter | appointment book | mechanical pencil |
| posture | organizer | swivel | timesheet |

Types of chairs:
- _____clerical_____
- _____
- _____

Things we write with:
- _____
- _____

Things we write in or on:
- _____
- _____

B. MATCHING: *ASSOCIATIONS*

_b_ **1.** rolodex   **a.** money

___ **2.** eraser   **b.** names and telephone numbers

___ **3.** pen   **c.** date

___ **4.** paycheck   **d.** holes

___ **5.** desk calendar   **e.** trash

___ **6.** wastebasket   **f.** cut

___ **7.** punch   **g.** mistake

___ **8.** scissors   **h.** ink

C. ANALOGIES

| staple remover | stamp pad | highlighter pen | pencils | typewriter |

1. pencil : eraser *as* _____typewriter_____ : correction fluid
2. memos : memo holder *as* _____ : pencil cup
3. swivel chair : chair *as* _____ : pen
4. eraser : pencil *as* _____ : stapler
5. personal planner : organizer *as* _____ : ink pad

D. WHICH WORD?

1. Where's my mechanical (eraser (pencil))?
2. Let me check my wall (pad   calendar).
3. I can't find my appointment (cards   book)!
4. I left your letter (opener   stamp) next to your mail.
5. How do you like your new file (desk   cabinet)?
6. My letter (remover   tray) is such a mess!
7. How do you put a new tape in the tape (wastebasket   dispenser)?
8. I have the rubber stamp, but I can't find the (desk   ink) pad.

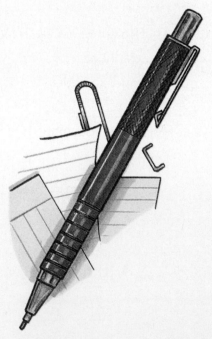

A. WHICH WORD?

1. I made a mistake on this letter. Do you have the (rubber cement (correction fluid))?

2. Don't staple the papers together. Use this (paper clip   sealing tape).

3. Write the telephone number on this (note pad   typewriter ribbon).

4. Please address this (thumb tack   mailing label).

5. The copier is broken. Please use (carbon paper   stationery) when you type the letter so we have an extra copy.

6. After you use the 3-hole punch, use three (paper fasteners   pushpins).

7. The gluestick doesn't work. Try some (typewriter ribbon   rubber cement).

8. Type this letter on our new (clamp   stationery).

9. We don't have any more mailers. Use a (mailing label   marker) and put it on a clasp envelope.

10. I need a (manila folder   catalog envelope) to start a new file.

B. WHICH WORD?

1. Write the names of all employees on this ((legal)   message) pad.

2. Hold all 50 timesheets together with a (binder   plastic) clip.

3. Do you know how to put the (computer   carbon) paper in the dot-matrix printer?

4. Write the name and telephone number on this small (legal   Post-It note) pad.

5. Masking tape isn't strong enough. Use this (cellophane   sealing) tape to send this package.

6. We're out of stationery. I have to use (typing   carbon) paper for this letter.

C. MATCHING: *WHAT DO WE USE IT FOR?*

<u>d</u> 1. paper clip

___ 2. computer paper

___ 3. message pad

___ 4. correction fluid

___ 5. pushpin

___ 6. rubber cement

___ 7. envelope

___ 8. mailing label

___ 9. carbon paper

a. to attach paper to a bulletin board

b. to glue pieces of paper together

c. to make a copy

d. to hold papers together

e. to cover a mistake

f. to write down messages

g. to print out information

h. to send a letter in the mail

i. to put an address on an envelope

Listen to the telephone conversations. Write the messages.

1.

To _Mr. Taylor_

Date _____ Time _____ ☐ AM ☐ PM

WHILE YOU WERE OUT

M _rs. Perez_

of _____

Phone _(212) 986-3098_
Area Code   Number   Extension

TELEPHONED	✔	PLEASE CALL	✔
CALLED TO SEE YOU		WILL CALL AGAIN	
WANTS TO SEE YOU		URGENT	
	RETURNED YOUR CALL		

Message _____
_____ _Call back today._ _____
_____
_____
_____
_____
_____

Operator

2.

To _Mr. Franco_

Date _____ Time _____ ☐ AM ☐ PM

WHILE YOU WERE OUT

M _r. White_

of _____

Phone _(   )_
Area Code   Number   Extension

TELEPHONED		PLEASE CALL	
CALLED TO SEE YOU		WILL CALL AGAIN	
WANTS TO SEE YOU		URGENT	
	RETURNED YOUR CALL		

Message _____
_____
_____
_____
_____
_____
_____

Operator

3.

To _Mrs. Ling_

Date _____ Time _____ ☐ AM ☐ PM

WHILE YOU WERE OUT

M _r. Ling_

of _____

Phone _(   )_
Area Code   Number   Extension

TELEPHONED		PLEASE CALL	
CALLED TO SEE YOU		WILL CALL AGAIN	
WANTS TO SEE YOU		URGENT	
	RETURNED YOUR CALL		

Message _____
_____
_____
_____
_____
_____
_____

Operator

4.

To _Ms. Benson_

Date _____ Time _____ ☐ AM ☐ PM

WHILE YOU WERE OUT

M _rs. Hobbs_

of _____

Phone _(   )_
Area Code   Number   Extension

TELEPHONED		PLEASE CALL	
CALLED TO SEE YOU		WILL CALL AGAIN	
WANTS TO SEE YOU		URGENT	
	RETURNED YOUR CALL		

Message _____
_____
_____
_____
_____
_____
_____

Operator

A. WHICH WORD?

1. I smell smoke!
   Get the ((fire extinguisher) time cards)!
2. I'm thirsty, but the cafeteria is closed.
   Let's get a drink from the (supply room   vending machine).
3. These boxes are very heavy.
   Use the (forklift   lever).
4. There's an accident on the second floor!
   Get the (first-aid kit   quality control supervisor)!
5. I have a problem with my paycheck.
   Talk to the secretary in the (suggestion box   payroll office).
6. Where are the safety glasses?
   In the (freight elevator   supply room).
7. I'm here for an interview.
   Go to the (loading dock   personnel office) on the second floor.
8. I have a question about my job.
   Ask your (foreman   worker).
9. I'm going home.
   Did you punch out your time (card   clock)?
10. The food in the cafeteria is terrible!
    Write a note and put it in the (suggestion box   assembly line).

B. MATCHING: *FINISH THE WORDS*

_c_	1.	union	a.	belt			6.	loading	f.	glasses
___	2.	work	b.	box		___	7.	supply	g.	extinguisher
___	3.	suggestion	c.	notice		___	8.	assembly	h.	room
___	4.	conveyor	d.	truck		___	9.	fire	i.	dock
___	5.	hand	e.	station		___	10.	safety	j.	line

C. WHICH WORD?

1. You can get a sandwich from the vending ((machine) box).
2. Load these boxes on the freight (elevator   machine).
3. The hand truck is at the shipping (dock   department).
4. The new employee is working at the loading (office   dock).
5. Take your time card to the personnel (department   office).

D. MATCHING: *DEFINITIONS*

_c_	1.	time card	a.	contains chemicals to put out fires
___	2.	safety glasses	b.	takes shipments up and down floors
___	3.	worker	c.	shows when the employee arrives and leaves
___	4.	fire extinguisher	d.	protects the eyes of the worker
___	5.	first-aid kit	e.	has bandages and bandaids
___	6.	payroll office	f.	is an employee
___	7.	freight elevator	g.	keeps paychecks for workers

A. WHICH GROUP?

brick	bulldozer	cement	crane	lumber	jackhammer
pickax	pickup truck	plywood	shovel	van	sledgehammer

Vehicles:
* _____
* _____
* _____
* _____

Tools:
* _____
* _____
* _____
* _____

Building materials:
* _____ brick _____
* _____
* _____
* _____

B. WHICH WORD?

1. Use that ((wheelbarrow)   scaffolding) to move the bricks!
2. Put on your (shingle   helmet) before you go to the construction site.
3. We don't have enough (level   plywood) to finish the job.
4. Please give me that (trowel   trailer).
5. Study the (blueprints   toolbelt) before you start the job.
6. Be careful when you come down the (ladder   shovel).
7. Are we going to have enough (sledgehammers   shingles) for the roof?
8. He operates that (bulldozer   girder) very well.

C. MATCHING: COMPOUND WORDS

Draw a line to the correct word. Then write the word on the line.

1. back   ax   _____ backhoe _____
2. blue   dozer   _____
3. bull   belt   _____
4. pick   prints   _____
5. sledge   hammer   _____
6. tool   hoe   _____
7. wheel   barrow   _____

D. LISTENING: WHAT ARE THEY TALKING ABOUT?

Listen and circle the correct word.

1. (beam)   brick   7. girder   tape measure
2. shovel   trowel   8. cherry picker   shingle
3. van   crane   9. bulldozer   front-end loader
4. blueprints   cement mixer   10. insulation   tape measure
5. wheelbarrow   backhoe   11. hardhats   pickax
6. level   trailer   12. pipe   wire

A. MATCHING: *WHAT SHOULD THEY USE?*

<u>h</u> 1. "Check the oil, please."

___ 2. "It's starting to rain."

___ 3. "I have to change the tire!"

___ 4. "Make a right."

___ 5. "Fill it up."

___ 6. "It's getting dark."

___ 7. "My battery is dead!"

___ 8. "I can't see out the back of the car!"

a. jack

b. jumper cables

c. gas tank

d. headlight

e. turn signal

f. rear defroster

g. windshield wipers

h. dipstick

B. MATCHING: *COMPOUND WORDS*

Draw a line to finish the word. Then write the word on the line.

1. tail   stick   <u>tailpipe</u>

2. head   cap   _____

3. hub   light   _____

4. sun   shield   _____

5. dash   pipe   _____

6. dip   roof   _____

7. wind   board   _____

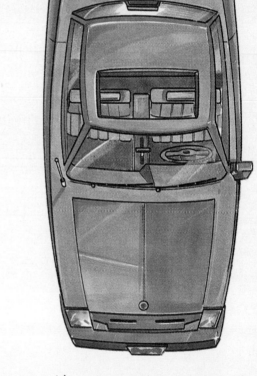

C. WHICH WORD?

1. Put on your turn (light (signal)).

2. Look in your side (pump mirror) before you pass.

3. Your license (rack plate) is falling off!

4. There's a problem with your fan (filter belt).

5. I have a spare (tire tank) in my trunk.

6. My windshield (rear wipers) aren't working.

7. You need oil. Look at this (dipstick muffler).

8. Be safe. Put your (tailpipe seat belt) on.

D. WHICH WORD?

1. The sun is bright. I can't see very well!
   Put the ((visor) accelerator) down.

2. The light is green! Why doesn't that driver go?
   Honk your (vent horn).

3. I can't start the car.
   I think the (ignition brake) is broken.

4. Did you buy a car with an automatic transmission?
   No. I prefer a car with a (stickshift headrest).

5. Where can I find a map?
   Look in the (glove compartment shoulder harness).

6. I need help. My car broke down.
   I'll send a (limousine tow truck).

E. MATCHING: *ASSOCIATIONS*

_d_ 1. speedometer   a. how much gas

___ 2. odometer   b. how hot or cold

___ 3. temperature gauge c. how far

___ 4. fuel gauge   d. how fast

___ 5. brake   e. open

___ 6. accelerator   f. stop

___ 7. door handle   g. turn

___ 8. steering wheel   h. go

___ 9. radio   i. sit

___10. seat   j. listen

F. SAFETY FIRST

| air bags | flares | jack | jumper cables | seat belts | spare tire | trunk |

As a good driver, you should always keep emergency equipment in the _____trunk_____ [1] of your car. When your battery doesn't work, you need to use _____ [2] and get help from another driver. In case of an emergency on the road, you can warn other drivers when you light your _____ [3] and put them on the street. When you have a flat tire, pull over. Make sure you stop in a safe area. Use your _____ [4] to lift your car. Replace the flat tire with a _____ [5]. You and your passengers should always use your _____ [6]. Some cars have _____ [7] to protect people in an accident.

G. LISTENING: *CHECKLIST*

Listen to the car dealers. Put a check next to the items each car has.

1.
- ✔ sunroof
- ___ luggage carrier
- ___ jack
- ___ spare tire
- ___ side mirror
- ___ cruise control
- ___ rear defroster
- ___ air bag
- ___ tape deck

2.
- ___ sunroof
- ___ luggage carrier
- ___ jack
- ___ spare tire
- ___ side mirror
- ___ cruise control
- ___ rear defroster
- ___ air bag
- ___ tape deck

A. WHICH WORD?

1. You didn't stop at the (route (stop)) sign.
2. You can get off the highway at the next (entrance exit) ramp.
3. Make a right turn at the next (shoulder intersection).
4. The (speed limit yield) sign says 55.
5. There's a (median crosswalk) at the next intersection.
6. We can buy gasoline at the (school crossing service area).
7. Pay 25¢ at the (barrier tollbooth).
8. Meet me at the (overpass corner) of Fifth Avenue and Elm Street.

B. MATCHING: *ASSOCIATIONS*

_f_ 1. tollbooth
___ 2. broken line
___ 3. exit sign
___ 4. solid line
___ 5. entrance ramp
___ 6. crosswalk

a. You can pass.
b. You can walk here.
c. You get on here.
d. You can't pass.
e. You get off here.
f. You pay here.

C. WHAT ARE THEY TALKING ABOUT?

| speed limit sign | tunnel | yield sign | tollbooth | school crossing | service area |

1. "Slow down. Watch for children."   _school crossing_
2. "Get some gas. Check the oil."   _____
3. "Slow down. Look carefully before you continue."   _____
4. "Do you have enough money?"   _____
5. "Don't go so fast!"   _____
6. "Turn your lights on before you enter."   _____

D. JOURNAL ENTRY

You witnessed an accident! The insurance company wants you to describe what happened. Draw a diagram and tell about the accident.

....
....
....
....
....

E. LISTENING: *TRAFFIC SIGNS*

Listen to the conversations. Write the number under the correct sign.

___   ___   1   ___   ___

A. WHERE DID THEY GO?

arrival and departure board	information booth	luggage	platform	porter
ticket window	timetable	track	train station	train

When we arrived at the _____train station_____ ¹, we first
went to the _____ ² to get a _____ ³
to see when the trains left. We decided to take the next _____ ⁴ to New York.
We bought our tickets at the _____ ⁵. According to
the _____ ⁶, our train was going to depart at 2:15 on
_____ ⁷ 18. It was 2:05! A _____ ⁸
carried our _____ ⁹ from the ticket window to the
_____ ¹⁰, and we got on the train.

We were on our way to New York!

B. WHICH WORD DOESN'T BELONG?

1. engineer   bus driver   (turnstile)   cab driver
2. token   passenger   commuter   rider
3. ticket   sleeper   token   fare card
4. track   bus stop   taxi stand   engine
5. sleeper   dining car   passenger car   porter
6. porter   conductor   transfer   passenger

C. WHICH WORD?

1. We're going to be riding all night. Let's get a ((sleeper)   platform).
2. How much is the (meter   fare) to the train station?
3. Don't leave the luggage on the (platform   transfer).
4. My aunt is going to meet us at the (engine   bus station).
5. The departure times are in the (turnstile   timetable).
6. Pay at the (information   token) booth.
7. The (engineer   redcap) will carry your baggage.
8. There was a line of passengers at the ticket (box   counter).

D. LISTENING: WHERE ARE THEY?

Listen to the conversations and decide where the passengers are.

___ on the train	___ in a subway station	___ in the dining car
___ in a taxi	_1_ on a bus	___ at an information booth

A. WHICH WORD?

1. Show your ticket to the agent at the ((check-in counter)   concession stand).
2. Let me help you with that (gate   suitcase).
3. All passengers have to go through the (metal detector   baggage carousel).
4. May I see your (ticket counter   boarding pass)?
5. Please take a seat in the (waiting area   check-in counter).
6. The (luggage carrier   skycap) will take your baggage to the ticket counter.
7. Please fill out your customs (declaration form   officer).
8. May I carry your (garment bag   porter)?

B. WHICH WORD DOESN'T BELONG?

1. ticket agent   (luggage carrier)   security guard   customs officer
2. immigration   baggage   suitcase   luggage
3. ticket   boarding pass   X-ray machine   claim check
4. X-ray machine   metal detector   baggage carousel   security guard
5. concession stand   gift shop   snack bar   immigration
6. ticket   gate   passport   visa

C. A TICKET

PASSENGER TICKET AND BAGGAGE CHECK
NOT TRANSFERRABLE

| FLIGHT COUPON | AGENT CODE | NAME OF PASSENGER |
| XXXXX | A39668005 | JOHNSON/JAMES |

ISSUED BY: UNITED AIRLINES   PLACE OF ISSUE: CHICAGO   DATE OF ISSUE: 12 MAY   FROM: CHICAGO

NAME OF PASSENGER: JOHNSON/JAMES   PHR/CARRIER CODE: QSXRCF/AA   SERV CARR ID: 0011/   TO: MADRID

X/O FROM CHICAGO   CARRIER UA   FLIGHT 723   CLASS V   DATE 05JUL   TIME 505PM*****   CARRIER: UNITED AIRLINES

X/O TO MADRID   ISSUING AGENT ID: EE6UAB5   CARR FL CL DATE TIME: UA 723V 05JUL505P

SEAT 16D   SMOKE NO   GATE   SEAT 16D   SMOKE NO

FARE/USD 778.00***************   ******
TAX 26.00****43551203146
TOTAL 804.00***************

CPN   DOCUMENT NUMBER   CK
NOT VALID
WITHOUT FLIGHT COUPON
ATTACHED

PCS WT UNCKD BAGGAGE ID #
****
****
AA39668005

1. What is the passenger's name?   _James Johnson_
2. Which airline is this passenger traveling on? ____
3. What is the date of departure? ____
4. What is the time of departure? ____
5. What city does the flight leave from? ____
6. Where is the passenger going? ____
7. What is the flight number? ____
8. How much does the ticket cost? ____
9. On what date did the passenger buy the ticket? ____

THE AIRPLANE

A. WHAT DO THEY NEED?

1. I feel nauseous. I think I'm going to be sick.
   Here. Use this (oxygen mask   (air sickness bag)).

2. How do I move my seat back?
   Use the (seat control   armrest).

3. Where can I wash my hands?
   The (lavatory   runway) is in the back of the plane.

4. Where can I put this carry-on bag?
   You can put it in the (overhead compartment   instrument panel).

5. I'm having trouble breathing!
   Put on this (galley   oxygen mask) and breathe slowly.

6. I'm looking for our flight attendant.
   I just saw him in the (seat pocket   galley).

B. WHICH WORD?

1. The co-pilot knows all the parts of the instrument ((panel)   instruction).
2. The sign says to fasten your seat (pocket   belt).
3. Where is the emergency (compartment   exit)?
4. The plane will taxi to the terminal (tower   building).
5. The pilot put down the landing (control   gear).
6. The captain and co-pilot sit in the (engine   nose) of the plane.

C. MATCHING: WHAT IS IT?

_d_ 1. terminal	a.	the bathroom
___ 2. nose	b.	the captain
___ 3. landing gear	c.	the motor
___ 4. lavatory	d.	the main building
___ 5. jet	e.	the wheels
___ 6. engine	f.	the front of the plane
___ 7. tail	g.	the airplane
___ 8. pilot	h.	the end of the plane

D. LISTENING

Listen and check the words you hear.

1.
- ___ seat belt
- ___ bathroom
- ___ life vest
- ___ call button
- ✔ oxygen mask
- ___ emergency exit
- ___ meal
- ___ emergency instruction card

2.
- ___ co-pilot
- ___ flight engineer
- ___ flight attendants
- ___ window seat
- ___ Fasten Seat Belt sign
- ___ meal
- ___ runway
- ___ control tower

3.
- ___ tray
- ___ oxygen mask
- ___ seat belt
- ___ seat control
- ___ landing gear
- ___ runway
- ___ terminal building
- ___ No Smoking sign

A. WHAT'S THE WORD?

snowing	foggy	raining	clear	windy

1. Take an umbrella. It's _____raining_____.
2. Be careful when you drive home. It's hard to see because it's so _____.
3. It's cold! I think it will be _____ soon.
4. There isn't a cloud in the sky. It's a _____ blue sky!
5. The leaves are blowing off the trees. It's really _____!

B. MATCHING: *ASSOCIATIONS*

_c_ 1. snowstorm   a. flashes of light in the sky

___ 2. lightning   b. very strong winds and rain

___ 3. thunderstorm   c. cold winds and snow

___ 4. hurricane   d. warm rain and noises in the sky

___ 5. winter   e. flowers bloom

___ 6. spring   f. leaves fall

___ 7. summer   g. cold temperatures

___ 8. autumn   h. hot temperatures

C. FAHRENHEIT AND CELSIUS

Look at the thermometer on page 98 of the Picture Dictionary. Read the sentence and choose the correct temperature.

1. "It's very hot today."   (a.) 90°F   b. 19°F
2. "It's very cold outside."   a. 80°F   b. 28°F
3. "It's a nice warm day."   a. 26°C   b. 5°C
4. "It's snowing."   a. -5°C   b. 5°C
5. "It's very hot today!"   a. 40°F   b. 40°C
6. "What a big snowstorm!"   a. 10°F   b. 10°C

D. LISTENING: *WEATHER FORECASTS*

Listen and write the number under the correct picture.

   _1_   ___   ___   ___

A. WHICH WORD?

1. We're going to be here all night. Did you bring your sleeping ((bag) boots)?
2. Where's the picnic (blanket   basket) for our drinks and sandwiches?
3. Let's put up the tent. Where are the (thermos   stakes)?
4. I don't want to get lost. Bring the compass and the (trail map   harness).
5. It's getting dark. Did you bring the (lantern   hatchet)?
6. I'm thirsty. Do you have the (compass   thermos)?
7. I can carry supplies in this (backpack   sleeping bag).
8. Hold on to the (rope   compass) with both hands.

B. MATCHING

_b_	1. hiking	a.	going up
___	2. on a picnic	b.	walking
___	3. climbing	c.	sleeping outside
___	4. camping	d.	eating

___	5. backpack	e.	cooking
___	6. hatchet	f.	light
___	7. lantern	g.	carrying
___	8. camp stove	h.	chopping

C. MATCHING

_d_	1. picnic	a.	bag
___	2. hiking	b.	stakes
___	3. trail	c.	boots
___	4. camp	d.	basket
___	5. tent	e.	stove
___	6. sleeping	f.	map

D. LISTENING: *WHERE ARE THEY GOING?*

Listen and write the number next to the correct word.

___ camping	___ hiking	_1_ rock climbing	___ on a picnic

THE PARK AND THE PLAYGROUND

A. WHICH WORD?

1. I'm going to get a drink at the (wading pool   (water fountain)).
2. Let's go see the animals (at the zoo   on the monkey bars).
3. Put your bike (on the grill   in the bike rack).
4. I'm going to run on the (merry-go-round   jogging path).
5. Please throw this away in the (sandbox   trash can).
6. Look at the horses on the (jungle gym   bridle path).
7. There is music every evening at the (rest rooms   band shell).
8. We can cook our food on the (grill   swings).

B. ANALOGIES

jogging path	tire swing	duck pond	rest rooms	bridle path	sandbox

1. water : wading pool *as* sand :   _____sandbox_____
2. bicycle : bikeway *as* horse :   _____
3. animals : zoo *as* ducks :   _____
4. merry-go-round : carousel *as* bathrooms :   _____
5. horses : bridle path *as* people :   _____
6. sit : bench *as* swing :   _____

C. WHAT ARE THEY TALKING ABOUT?

statue	seesaw	bench	water fountain	duck pond	jungle gym	rest rooms	zoo

1. "Don't climb up there so high!"   _____jungle gym_____
2. "Be careful! Don't fall in!"   _____
3. "Take a drink!"   _____
4. "Up and down! Up and down!"   _____
5. "Sit down here and rest for a minute!"   _____
6. "Do you have to go to the bathroom?"   _____
7. "Look at all the animals!"   _____
8. "Who's that?"   _____

D. LISTENING: *WHAT ARE THEY TALKING ABOUT?*

Listen and circle the correct word.

1. (jungle gym)   wading pool   5. bike rack   sandbox
2. trash can   rest room   6. fountain   duck pond
3. playground   merry-go-round   7. trash can   sand
4. picnic area   bikeway   8. carousel   band shell

A. MATCHING: *WHAT DO THEY DO?*

_c_ **1.** lifeguard
___ **2.** surfer
___ **3.** vendor
___ **4.** sunbather

a. sells drinks and snacks
b. sits in the sun
c. saves swimmers
d. rides the waves

___ **5.** sunglasses
___ **6.** cooler
___ **7.** bathing cap
___ **8.** sunscreen

e. keeps hair dry
f. protect the eyes
g. protects the skin
h. keeps drinks cold

B. WHICH WORD?

1. When I'm at the beach, I always sit under a ((beach umbrella) cooler).
2. The sun is very bright! I need my (sand castle   sunglasses).
3. It's really windy! What a good day to fly a (surfboard   kite)!
4. Let's sit down on this (shovel   blanket).
5. I'm going to the (sand dune   refreshment stand) to get a drink.
6. Let's throw the (beach ball   snack bar) around.
7. I bought a new (swimsuit   rock).
8. Use a (bucket   towel) to make a sand castle.
9. The lifeguard is a very strong (sunbather   swimmer).
10. The surfers are happy about the big (pails   waves).

C. ANALOGIES

raft	wave	lifeguard stand	kite	bathing cap	swimsuit

1. sunbather : sun hat *as* swimmer : _____ bathing cap _____
2. pail : bucket *as* bathing suit : _____
3. wave : surfboard *as* wind : _____
4. sunbather : beach chair *as* lifeguard : _____
5. seashell : shell *as* air mattress : _____
6. sand : dune *as* water : _____

D. LISTENING: *WHAT ARE THEY TALKING ABOUT?*

1. (chair)   shovel
2. raft   kite
3. tube   bathing cap
4. shovel   towel
5. swimsuit   sunscreen
6. vendor   surfer
7. blanket   sun hat
8. life preserver   sunbather

A. WHAT ARE THEY?

bowling shoes	boxing gloves	darts	frisbee
handball glove	jogging shoes	walking shoes	

Things you throw:

_____

_____

Things you wear on your feet:

_____bowling shoes_____

_____

_____

Things you wear on your hands:

_____

_____

B. MATCHING: ASSOCIATIONS

__d__ 1. ping pong   a. glove

____ 2. skydiving   b. ball

____ 3. bowling   c. airplane

____ 4. boxing   d. net

____ 5. skateboarding   e. saddle

____ 6. wrestling   f. elbow pad

____ 7. horseback riding   g. mat

C. WHICH WORD?

1. Put your feet in the ((stirrups) safety goggles).

2. Put on your (saddle   helmet) before you go biking.

3. Protect your eyes with (parachutes   safety goggles).

4. Throw the (frisbee   dart) to me!

5. Peter lifts (ping pong balls   weights) every day.

6. Kathy likes to jump on the (target   trampoline).

7. Please hand me the pool (table   stick).

8. Tom likes to practice with a bow and (ball   arrow).

9. My new wrestling (uniform   mat) doesn't fit!

10. I wear my (handball   boxing) glove on my left hand.

D. ANALOGIES

archery	billiard balls	skydiving	roller skating	golf club	paddle

1. squash ball : squash racquet *as* ping pong ball : _____paddle_____

2. tennis ball : golf ball *as* tennis racquet : _____

3. elbow pads : skateboarding *as* knee pads : _____

4. dartboard : darts *as* target : _____

5. trampoline : gymnastics *as* parachute : _____

6. tennis : tennis balls *as* pool : _____

A. WHICH SPORTS?

Look carefully at the pictures on page 104 of the Picture Dictionary and answer the questions.

1. In which sports do players wear something on their heads?

_____baseball_____   _____   _____

_____   _____

2. Which sport uses a ball that isn't round? _____

3. Which sports are played on a field?

_____   _____   _____

_____   _____

4. Which sport is played on a rink? _____

B. CROSSWORD

ACROSS

1.

4.

5.

6.

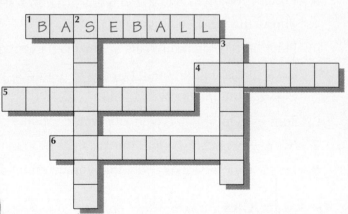

DOWN

2.

3.

A. MATCHING: *ASSOCIATIONS*

_e_ 1. softball
___ 2. football
___ 3. hockey
___ 4. soccer
___ 5. volleyball
___ 6. lacrosse
___ 7. basketball
___ 8. baseball

a. skates, stick, mask
b. hoop, backboard
c. face guard, stick, ball
d. shinguards, goal
e. glove, softball
f. bat, helmet, glove, mitt
g. helmet, shoulder pads
h. net, volleyball

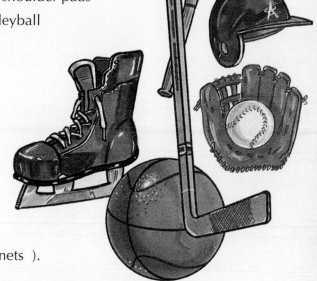

B. WHICH WORD?

1. I'm batting next. Where's the batting (stick (helmet))?
2. Put on the hockey (puck   mask) to protect your face.
3. That player dropped the hockey (skate   stick)!
4. The basketball went in the (glove   hoop).
5. Football players must wear (mitts   helmets).
6. I can't find my softball (glove   shinguards).
7. Hit the puck with the (hockey   lacrosse) stick.
8. All the players on our team are wearing new (uniforms   nets).

C. WHICH WORD DOESN'T BELONG?

1. catcher's mask   hockey mask   face guard   (shinguard)
2. bat   lacrosse ball   hockey puck   soccer ball
3. hockey stick   bat   backboard   lacrosse stick
4. baseball glove   shoulder pads   hockey glove   catcher's mitt
5. basketball   football   volleyball   hockey

⊡ D. LISTENING: *WHICH SPORT IS IT?*

Listen to the radio announcer and write the number next to the correct picture.

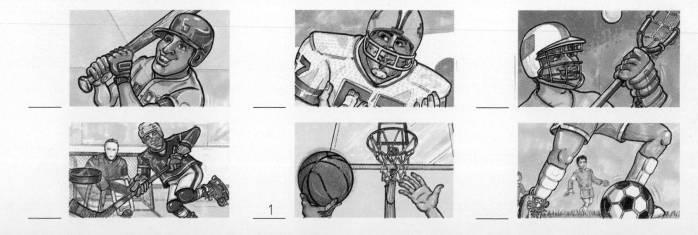

A. WHICH SPORTS?

Look carefully at the pictures on page 106 of the Picture Dictionary and answer the questions.

1. For which sports do you use poles?

   _____downhill skiing_____   _____

2. Which sports do you do on ice?

   _____   _____

3. For which activity do you need gasoline for your motor? _____

4. Which sports and activities do you do sitting down?

   _____   _____

   _____   _____

B. MATCHING: *WHERE?*

_c_ **1.** downhill skiing   **a.** on an ice rink

___ **2.** cross-country skiing   **b.** through a field or woods noisily

___ **3.** skating   **c.** down a mountain, standing up

___ **4.** sledding   **d.** through a field or woods quietly

___ **5.** snowmobile   **e.** down a hill, sitting down

C. WHICH WORD?

1. We go downhill skiing without ((poles)   bindings)!
2. My daughter practices figure (skating   skiing) every day.
3. We can go across the mountain easily with the (saucer   snowmobile).
4. My friends are on the Olympic (sledding   bobsledding) team.
5. Don't fall off the (toboggan   bindings)!
6. (Downhill   Cross-country) skiing is so calm and peaceful.

D. MATCHING: *DEFINITIONS*

_b_ **1.** We use these to protect the bottom of skates.   **a.** saucer

___ **2.** We use these to attach ski boots to skis.   **b.** skate guards

___ **3.** This is a round type of sled.   **c.** poles

___ **4.** This is a vehicle with a motor.   **d.** bindings

___ **5.** We use these to help us keep balance.   **e.** snowmobile

WATER SPORTS AND RECREATION

A. WHICH WORD?

1. The waves are big! Get your (snorkel (surfboard))!

2. The towrope broke while I was (figure skating   waterskiing).

3. I need some bait before I go (sailing   fishing).

4. Do you have your (mask   oars) for snorkeling?

5. I always go (surfing   fishing) in this pond.

6. Use this life preserver when you go (scuba diving   sailing).

B. MATCHING: *ASSOCIATIONS*

<u>d</u> **1.** goggles

___ **2.** snorkel

___ **3.** flippers

___ **4.** life jacket

___ **5.** bathing cap

a. feet

b. chest

c. head

d. eyes

e. mouth

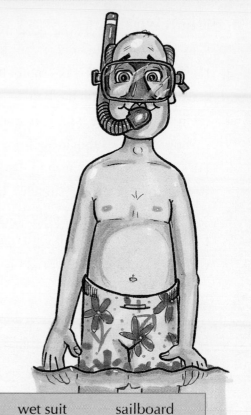

C. ANALOGIES

flippers	swimsuit	air tank	paddles	wet suit	sailboard

1. oars : rowboat *as* _____paddles_____ : canoe

2. waterskis : waterskiing *as* _____ : windsurfing

3. bathing suit : swimming *as* _____ : scuba diving

4. goggles : eyes *as* _____ : feet

5. snorkel : snorkeling *as* _____ : scuba diving

6. wet suit : diving mask *as* _____ : goggles

D. LISTENING: *WHAT ARE THEY DOING?*

Listen and write the number under the correct picture.

___

___

___

<u>1</u>

___

___

SPORT AND EXERCISE ACTIONS

A. WHICH WORD?

1. Can you ((bend) shoot) your knee?
2. He can (lift   pass) the football very far!
3. (Dribble   Reach) the ball!
4. (Lie down   Dive) into the deep part of the pool.
5. (Shoot   Push) the arrow from the bow.
6. Let's (run   catch) around the jogging path.
7. Before you exercise, (stretch   bounce) your legs.
8. (Jump   Swing) your arms up and down.
9. (Hit   Throw) the ball with the bat.
10. (Hop   Kneel) on your right foot ten times.

B. ANALOGIES

kneel	hop	baseball	hands	shoot	throw

1. hit : baseball *as* _____shoot_____ : basketball
2. kick : soccer *as* _____ : baseball
3. tennis : serve *as* _____ : pitch
4. feet : hop *as* _____ : cartwheel
5. walk: run *as* _____ : jump
6. reach : hands *as* _____ : knees

C. MATCHING: *ASSOCIATIONS*

_e_ 1. kick   a. tennis
___ 2. pitch   b. basketball
___ 3. shoot   c. volleyball
___ 4. pass   d. baseball
___ 5. serve   e. football

D. LISTENING: *AEROBICS*

Listen and put the number under the correct picture.

____   ____   ____   1   ____   ____

HANDICRAFTS, HOBBIES, AND GAMES

A. WHAT'S THE WORD?

pottery	astronomy	sewing	coin collecting
painting	games	photography	woodworking

1. My son likes to build things. His hobby is _____woodworking_____.
2. Janet takes wonderful pictures. She likes _____.
3. My mother makes all her clothes. She's very good at _____.
4. We bought David an easel. He enjoys _____.
5. The moon is clear tonight! I like _____!
6. What do you want to play? I have a lot of different _____.
7. What kind of clay do you use to make your _____?
8. My uncle has money from all over the world. He really enjoys _____.

B. MATCHING: *ASSOCIATIONS*

_c_ 1. knitting   a. bowls
___ 2. painting   b. clothes
___ 3. pottery   c. sweaters
___ 4. weaving   d. rugs
___ 5. sewing   e. pictures

C. ANALOGIES

knitting	binoculars	bird watching	knitting needle	coin album

1. stamps : stamp album *as* coins : _____coin album_____
2. thread : sewing *as* yarn : _____
3. crocheting : knitting *as* crochet hook : _____
4. coin catalog : coin collecting *as* field guide : _____
5. astronomy : telescope *as* birdwatching : _____

D. WHAT ARE THEY TALKING ABOUT?

astronomy	bird watching	coin collecting	Scrabble	sewing

1. "It's a very rare dime. It's from 1927."   _____coin collecting_____
2. "Can you see the North Star?" _____
3. "My needle broke!" _____
4. "Look at the color of those feathers!" _____
5. "I'm not sure how to spell this word!" _____

A. WHICH WORD?

1. It was a good movie. The ((audience) chorus) clapped at the end.
2. The (spotlight orchestra) was on the opera singer as she sang.
3. I'll wait for you in the (refreshment stand lobby).
4. We couldn't see well. We sat in the (podium balcony).
5. She dances for a very good ballet (slipper company).
6. You can get your (tickets toeshoes) at the box office.
7. The singing of the (musicians chorus) was wonderful.
8. The musicians followed the (baton podium) of the conductor.

B. MATCHING

_d_ **1.** orchestra   **a.** office
___ **2.** symphony   **b.** singer
___ **3.** opera   **c.** orchestra
___ **4.** ballet   **d.** pit
___ **5.** box   **e.** dancer

C. WHICH WORD DOESN'T BELONG?

1. mezzanine   (usher)   stage   podium
2. actress   ballerina   opera singer   billboard
3. chorus   toeshoes   audience   musicians
4. ballet company orchestra   chorus   ballerina
5. balcony   ticket   mezzanine   orchestra
6. ballerina   conductor   ballet dancer   dancer

D. WHO IS TALKING?

Write the correct word.

| actress | ballerina | conductor | musician | usher |

1. I love to work for this conductor!

musician

2. May I see your ticket, please?

_____

3. My toes hurt!

_____

4. How can I perform with this sore throat?

_____

5. You aren't playing together. Watch the baton, please.

_____

A. WHO LIKES WHAT?

TV programs	music	play	movies

I like to go out on Friday and Saturday nights. I like to go to concerts to listen to _____music_____ [1]

or go to the theater to see a _____ [2].

My brother doesn't like to go out on weekends. He's happy to stay home, sit in the living room, and

watch his favorite _____ [3].

My big sister likes to stay home, too. She rents _____ [4] and watches them on the VCR!

We never do anything together!

B. LISTENING: *WHAT TYPE OF MUSIC IS IT?*

Listen to the music. Put the number next to the correct type of music.

___ classical	_1_ rap music	___ country	___ rock
___ gospel	___ jazz	___ reggae	

C. WHAT TYPE OF MOVIE IS IT?

Write the correct word.

cartoon	comedy	foreign
war		western

1. "I'm gonna get that rabbit if it's the last thing I do!"   _____cartoon_____
2. "Hey, cowboy!"   _____
3. "The enemy is here! The fighting will begin soon."   _____
4. "Non possiamo vivere cosi. Scappiamo subito."   _____
5. "Ha, ha, ha!"   _____

D. WHAT TYPE OF TV PROGRAM IS IT?

news program	game show	sports show
children's show	talk show	music video

1. "So, what's the name of your next movie?"   _____talk show_____
2. "And the winner of today's show is . . . "   _____
3. "A, B, C, D, E, F, G, . . . "   _____
4. "Good evening. This is Thursday, November 11, 1995."   _____
5. "And next, here's the latest song from Aerosmith."   _____
6. "The score is 2 to zero. . . "   _____

MUSICAL INSTRUMENTS

A. WHICH WORD DOESN'T BELONG?

1. synthesizer	(banjo)	organ	piano
2. harp	mandolin	viola	accordion
3. trumpet	bassoon	recorder	piccolo
4. guitar	ukelele	clarinet	bass
5. drum	xylophone	conga	harmonica

B. CROSSWORD

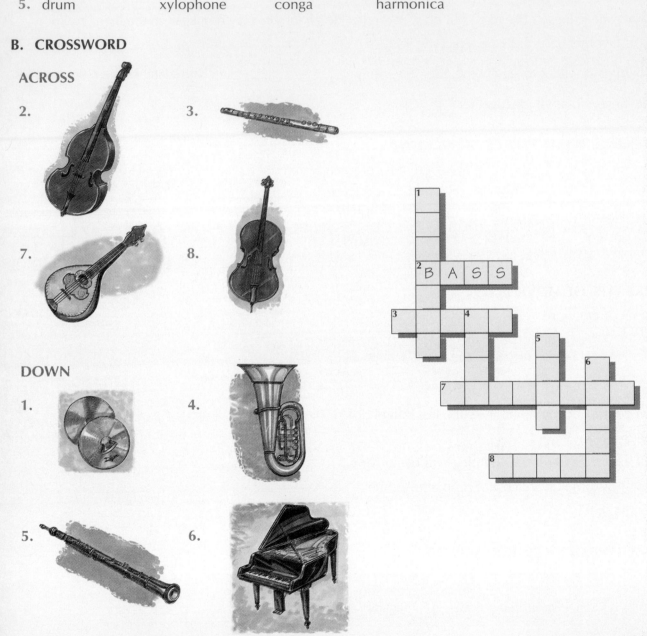

ACROSS

2.

3.

7.

8.

DOWN

1.

4.

5.

6.

C. LISTENING: *WHICH INSTRUMENT IS IT?*

Listen to the music. Write the number next to the correct instrument.

___ tuba	___ drum	___ flute
_1_ harmonica	___ harp	___ banjo

TREES, FLOWERS, AND PLANTS

A. WHAT'S THE WORD?

| branch | maple | tulips | leaves | palm | grass |

1. I like the different colors of ____leaves____ in the fall.
2. During the storm a big _____ from a tree fell on my car.
3. I cut the _____ every Saturday afternoon.
4. The _____ leaf is a symbol on the Canadian flag.
5. Many colorful types of _____ come from the Netherlands.
6. Look at all the coconuts on that _____ tree!

B. MATCHING: ASSOCIATIONS

_b_ 1. cactus   a. cone
___ 2. rose   b. desert
___ 3. pine   c. rash
___ 4. grass   d. thorn
___ 5. poison ivy   e. lawnmower

C. ANALOGIES

| bulb | flower | cactus |
| trunk | sunflower | |

1. stem : flower as ____trunk____ : tree
2. tree : maple as _____ : lily
3. leaf : leaves as _____ : cacti
4. root : elm as _____ : tulip
5. flower : tree as _____ : redwood

D. CROSSWORD

ACROSS

1.

2.

4.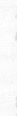

5.

7.

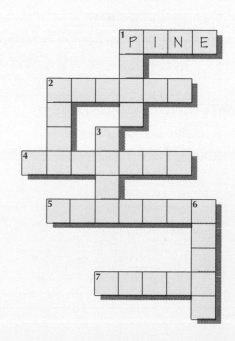

DOWN

1.

2.

3.

6.

A. WHICH WORD?

1. We're going to take our canoe down the (waterfall (river)).
2. Let's take a hike in the (forest   pond).
3. Do you heat your house with (oil   radiation)?
4. There's a farm in the (valley   desert) between the two mountains.
5. They went fishing in the (water pollution   brook).
6. It isn't a mountain. It's just a little (dam   hill).
7. The factory closed because of its (toxic waste   solar energy).
8. Don't go too close to the (dune   cliff)! You'll fall off!

B. WHICH WORD DOESN'T BELONG?

1. stream   brook   river   (desert)
2. meadow   rapids   field   valley
3. bay   oil   gas   coal
4. island   desert   valley   ocean
5. waterfall   pond   hill   rapids
6. toxic waste   solar energy   acid rain   water pollution
7. seashore   jungle   forest   woods

C. MATCHING: WHAT'S THE PLACE?

_b_ 1. a hot and dry place   a. plateau
___ 2. a place with trees and animals   b. desert
___ 3. high and flat land   c. ocean
___ 4. water with waves   d. forest
___ 5. a hill of sand   e. dune

D. MATCHING: ASSOCIATIONS

_d_ 1. solar energy   a. toxic waste
___ 2. hydroelectric power   b. radiation
___ 3. air pollution   c. cars
___ 4. nuclear energy   d. sunshine
___ 5. water pollution   e. waterfalls

E. JOURNAL ENTRY

List three ways people can protect the environment.

1. ....
2. ....
3. ....

A. WHICH WORD?

1. Give the horses ((hay)   turkey) to eat.

2. I'm growing tomatoes, peppers, and corn in my (crop   garden).

3. Let's make a (fence   scarecrow) to keep the birds away.

4. Our garden gets enough water with our new (hired hand   irrigation system).

5. Please hand me that (orchard   pitchfork).

6. The calves are in the (farmhouse   barnyard).

7. Take the (turkeys   sheep) to the pasture.

8. We keep the supplies in the (combine   barn).

B. ANALOGIES

calf	chicken	farmer	goat	hen	horse	piglet

1. bull : cow *as* rooster : _____hen_____

2. hen house : chicken *as* stable : _____

3. lamb : sheep *as* kid : _____

4. pig sty : chicken coop *as* pig : _____

5. barn : farm animal *as* farmhouse : _____

6. chicken : chick *as* pig : _____

7. goat : cow *as* kid : _____

C. MATCHING: *ASSOCIATIONS*

_e_ 1. chicken   a. milk

___ 2. cow   b. fruit

___ 3. orchard   c. help

___ 4. irrigation system d. animals

___ 5. hired hand   e. eggs

___ 6. scarecrow   f. water

___ 7. barn   g. morning

___ 8. rooster   h. birds

D. LISTENING: *WHICH ANIMAL IS IT?*

Listen to the sounds of farm animals. Write the number of the sound on the correct line.

___ horse	___ rooster	_1_ turkey
___ lamb	___ pig	___ goat
___ chick	___ cow	

A. WHICH WORD?

1. We gave her a (slug   (kitten)) for her birthday.

2. Different types of zebras have different types of (horns   stripes).

3. It's time to feed the (worm   gerbil).

4. This sweater is made from the wool of the (llama   rhinoceros).

5. Do you want to ride the (hyena   pony)?

6. Look at the (bison   squirrel) in that tree!

7. Let's go see the (monkeys   rats) at the zoo.

8. Every morning I take my (puppy   chipmunk) for a walk.

B. MATCHING: *WHICH ANIMAL IS IT?*

_e_	1. beaver	a. It *throws* its quills.
___	2. skunk	b. Its odor is unpleasant.
___	3. hyena	c. It sleeps upside down.
___	4. bat	d. Its kids are in its pouch.
___	5. porcupine	e. Its teeth are very strong.
___	6. kangaroo	f. Its laugh is like a human's.

___	7. anteater	g. It's from Australia.
___	8. polar bear	h. It uses its hands like a human.
___	9. koala	i. It's from China.
___	10. chimpanzee	j. It lives in the ground.
___	11. worm	k. It lives at the North Pole.
___	12. panda	l. It eats insects.

C. ANALOGIES

dog	quills	wolf	foal	gibbon
rhinoceros	mouse	lion	beaver	zebra

1. fawn : deer *as* _____foal_____ : horse

2. elephant : tusk *as* _____ : horn

3. wolf : wolves *as* _____ : mice

4. leopard : spots *as* _____ : stripes

5. horse : tail *as* _____ : mane

6. camel : desert *as* _____ : river

7. cat : kitten *as* _____ : puppy

8. whiskers : cat *as* _____ : porcupine

9. mouse : hamster *as* _____ : baboon

10. cat : mouse *as* _____ : rabbit

D. WHICH WORD DOESN'T BELONG?

1. horse   foal   (raccoon)   pony
2. mice   wolves   rats   guinea pigs
3. antler   buffalo   tusk   horn
4. pouch   quill   whiskers   tail
5. panda   koala   gorilla   grizzly bear
6. kitten   puppy   foal   mouse
7. hamster   armadillo   dog   gerbil

E. MATCHING: *WHAT DO THEY EAT?*

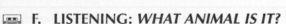

_b_ 1. mice	a. leaves of tall trees
___ 2. squirrels	b. cheese
___ 3. bats	c. grass and bark
___ 4. deer	d. fish
___ 5. horses	e. insects
___ 6. giraffes	f. nuts and seeds
___ 7. polar bears	g. soil
___ 8. worms	h. hay

F. LISTENING: *WHAT ANIMAL IS IT?*

Listen and circle the correct word.

1. rat   (bat)   6. foal   fawn
2. mouse   moose   7. monkey   donkey
3. bison   lion   8. anteater   beaver
4. raccoon   kangaroo   9. polar bear koala bear
5. hyena   zebra   10. leopard   gopher

G. MAKING COMPARISONS

| pig | owl | fox | cow | bear | bat | beaver | mouse | bull | donkey |

1. as hungry as a _____bear_____   6. as big as a _____
2. as sly as a _____   7. as quiet as a _____
3. as stubborn as a _____   8. as wise as an _____
4. as fat as a _____   9. as blind as a _____
5. as strong as a _____   10. as busy as a _____

H. LISTENING: *WHICH ANIMAL IS IT?*

Listen to the sounds of animals and pets. Write the number of the sound on the correct line.

___ mouse	___ wolf	___ donkey	___ lion	___ cat
_1_ bear	___ hyena	___ elephant	___ gorilla	___ dog

115

BIRDS AND INSECTS

A. WHICH BIRD?

Look at page 118 of the Picture Dictionary and circle the correct word.

1. A bird with excellent eyesight that comes out at night is the ((owl)   sparrow).
2. The smallest bird is the (pheasant   hummingbird).
3. A bird that usually lives in the city is the (pigeon   hawk).
4. A bird that can learn to speak is the (ostrich   parrot).
5. A bird that doesn't fly is the (cardinal   penguin).
6. The bird with feathers that look like many *eyes* is the (woodpecker   peacock).
7. The bird that is the symbol of the United States is the (crow   eagle).

B. WHICH INSECT?

Look at page 118 of the Picture Dictionary and circle the correct word.

1. The insect with eight legs is the (ant   (spider)).
2. The insect that shines a light at night is the (firefly   wasp).
3. The insect that makes dogs scratch is the (beetle   flea).
4. The insect that becomes a butterfly is the (centipede   caterpillar).
5. The insect that eats wood is the (termite   ladybug).
6. The insect that drinks blood is the (moth   tick).
7. The insect that makes honey is the (butterfly   bee).
8. The insect that *sings* in the evenings is the (lightning bug   cricket).

C. ANALOGIES

feather	woodpecker	web	bill	cockroach	nest

1. beehive : bee *as* _____nest_____ : robin
2. beak : woodpecker *as* _____ : duck
3. firefly : lightning bug *as* _____ : roach
4. nest : bird *as* _____ : spider
5. hummingbird : flower *as* _____ : wood
6. wing : butterfly *as* _____ : peacock

D. LISTENING: *SOUNDS*

Listen to the sounds of birds and insects. Write the number next to the correct word.

___ crow	___ woodpecker	_1_ cricket	___ duck
___ seagull	___ owl	___ parrot	___ bee

116

FISH, SEA ANIMALS, AND REPTILES

A. MATCHING: *ASSOCIATIONS*

_b_	1.	eel	a.	swimmer's enemy
___	2.	octopus	b.	electric
___	3.	turtle	c.	eight
___	4.	tadpole	d.	friendly
___	5.	shark	e.	slow-moving
___	6.	dolphin	f.	baby frog

B. ANALOGIES

claw	seal	snake	starfish	mussels	alligator	lizard

1. fish : bass *as* _____snake_____ : cobra
2. salmon : fish *as* _____ : reptile
3. turtle : tortoise *as* _____ : crocodile
4. tentacle : octopus *as* _____ : lobster
5. trout : salmon *as* _____ : oysters
6. octopus : eight *as* _____ : five
7. fish : tail *as* _____ : flipper

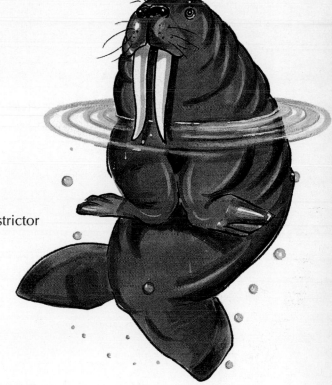

C. WHICH WORD DOESN'T BELONG?

1. (seal)   tail   gill   fin
2. rattlesnake   walrus   cobra   boa constrictor
3. clam   mussel   scallop   whale
4. flounder   lobster   squid   shrimp
5. lobster   eel   shrimp   crab
6. crab   seal   walrus   otter
7. jellyfish   snail   iguana   squid
8. tadpole   tusk   claw   shell

D. JOURNAL ENTRY

Which fish, sea animals, and reptiles do people commonly eat in your country? How do they prepare them? Which ones do you like? Which ones don't you like? Why?

....

....

....

....

....

....

A. WHICH HAS THE SAME MEANING?

_b_ **1.** How wide is it?

____ **2.** How tall is it?

____ **3.** How deep is it?

____ **4.** How long is it?

____ **5.** How far is it?

a. What's the distance?

b. What's the width?

c. What's the length?

d. What's the height?

e. What's the depth?

B. ANALOGIES

square	wide	ellipse	diameter	triangle	meter	depth

1. length : long *as* _____*depth*_____ : deep

2. foot : mile *as* _____ : kilometer

3. circle : cone *as* _____ : pyramid

4. square : four *as* _____ : three

5. rectangle: square *as* _____ : circle

6. diagonal : rectangle *as* _____ : circle

7. high: height *as* _____ : width

C. MATCHING: *ABBREVIATIONS*

_c_ **1.** centimeter

____ **2.** foot

____ **3.** yard

____ **4.** mile

____ **5.** inch

____ **6.** kilometer

____ **7.** meter

a. yd.

b. mi.

c. cm

d. "

e. km

f. m

g. '

D. WHAT DOES IT EQUAL?

foot	mile	inch	yard

1. 1.6 km   1 ____*mile*____

2. 2.54 cm   1 _____

3. 0.914 m   1 _____

4. 0.305 m   1 _____

A. DO YOU REMEMBER?

U.S. schoolchildren sometimes memorize the names of the nine planets by learning:

"My Very Energetic Mother Just Served Us Nine Pizzas."

Without looking in the Picture Dictionary, can you write the names of the nine planets in the correct order?

M: _____Mercury_____   M: _____   U: _____

V: _____   J: _____   N: _____

E: _____   S: _____   P: _____

B. MATCHING

_d_ **1.** lunar   **a.** pad

___ **2.** space   **b.** control

___ **3.** launch   **c.** shuttle

___ **4.** booster   **d.** eclipse

___ **5.** mission   **e.** rocket

C. CROSSWORD: *PICTURES TO WORDS*

ACROSS

2.    5.

7.    8.

9.

DOWN

1. 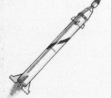   3.

4.    6.

Crossword grid:
2 ACROSS: C O N S T E L L A T I O N

WORKBOOK PAGE 1

A. WHAT'S THE WORD?

1. first	5. apartment
2. family	6. zip
3. phone	7. area
4. social security	

B. WHAT'S THE ANSWER?

1. d	5. h
2. c	6. e
3. a	7. g
4. b	8. f

WORKBOOK PAGE 2

A. WHICH GROUP?

wife	husband
mother	father
daughter	son
sister	brother
niece	nephew

B. HIS NAME OR HER NAME?

1. Her	4. His
2. His	5. His
3. Her	6. Her

C. WHO IS WHO?

1. e	4. a
2. f	5. c
3. d	6. b

D. IN OTHER WORDS

1. mother	3. grandfather
2. father	4. grandmother

WORKBOOK PAGES 3-4

A. WHICH GROUP?

aunt	cousin	uncle
niece		nephew
mother-in-law		father-in-law
daughter-in-law		son-in-law
sister-in-law		brother-in-law

B. WHICH WORD?

1. aunt, her	4. niece, Her
2. He's, he	5. uncle, cousin
3. His, nephew	6. she, husband

C. WHAT'S THE WORD?

1. sister	4. brother
2. father	5. son
3. mother	6. daughter

D. AT PAT AND JIM'S WEDDING

1. wife	7. nephew
2. sister	8. son
3. husband	9. sister
4. parents	10. niece
5. father	11. brother
6. mother	

WORKBOOK PAGE 5

A. USING A COMPASS

	north
northwest	northeast
west	east
southwest	southeast
	south

B. USING THE MAP: *THE U.S.A.*

1. c	4. a
2. d	5. b
3. e	6. f

C. WHICH STATES?

1. North Carolina, North Dakota
2. South Carolina, South Dakota
3. West Virginia

D. CENTRAL AMERICA AND THE CARIBBEAN

1. Nicaragua	4. Jamaica
2. Costa Rica	5. Dominican Republic
3. Mexico	6. Guatemala

WORKBOOK PAGE 6

A. WHICH CONTINENT

South America:	Europe:	Asia:	Africa:
Argentina	Austria	China	Egypt
Brazil	Germany	Japan	Nigeria
Chile	France	Korea	Zaire

B. A TRIP AROUND THE WORLD

1. Atlantic	4. Pacific
2. Mediterranean	5. Arctic
3. Indian	

WORKBOOK PAGE 7

A. WHAT DO THEY DO?

1. get	7. brushes
2. takes	8. washes
3. shaves	9. puts on
4. combs	10. makes
5. get	11. say
6. have	12. go

B. CROSSWORD: *PICTURES AND WORDS (see p. 145)*

C. CROSSWORD: *WHAT DO WE DO? (see p. 145)*

D. WHAT'S THE SEQUENCE?

5
1
3
4
2
6

E. LISTENING: *EVERYDAY SOUNDS*

Listen to the sounds. Write the number next to the activity.

1. (Sound: bath)
2. (Sound: shower)
3. (Sound: making dinner)
4. (Sound: brushing teeth)
5. (Sound: electric shaver)

Answers

2
4
1
3
5

WORKBOOK PAGE 8

A. WHICH WORD?

1. floor	6. dog
2. dishes	7. floor
3. piano	8. radio
4. play	9. TV
5. iron	10. house

B. MATCHING

1. d
2. b
3. c
4. a
5. f
6. e

C. WHAT'S THE ACTION?

listen to   do   iron   watch
     feed   read   play

D. LISTEN: *MORE EVERYDAY SOUNDS*

Listen to the sounds. Put the number of each sound next to the correct sentence.

1. (Sound: washing machine)
2. (Sound: basketball bouncing)
3. (Sound: radio)
4. (Sound: exercising/counting)
5. (Sound: broom sweeping floor)
6. (Sound: vacuum cleaner)
7. (Sound: feeding baby)
8. (Sound: washing dishes)
9. (Sound: guitar)
10. (Sound: piano)

Answers

5	4
1	10
6	9
8	2
7	3

WORKBOOK PAGE 9

A. WHERE ARE THE THINGS?

1. globe
2. overhead
3. clock
4. eraser
5. calculator
6. ruler

B. MATCHING

1. f
2. e
3. a
4. b
5. c
6. d

C. MATCHING: *COMPOUND WORDS*

1. textbook
2. loudspeaker
3. thumbtack
4. bookshelf

D. HOW DO WE USE THEM?

1. chalk
2. a pencil
3. a bookshelf
4. a thumbtack
5. a ruler
6. a calculator

WORKBOOK PAGE 10

A. THE TEACHER'S INSTRUCTIONS

1. hand
2. mistake
3. homework
4. test
5. papers
6. the shade
7. the answer
8. question
9. groups
10. the light

B. WHAT'S THE SEQUENCE?

5
2
4
6
1
3

C. WHAT ARE THEY DOING?

1. She's writing her name.
2. She's raising her hand.
3. He's putting away his book.
4. He's handing in his homework.
5. They're watching the movie.
6. He's taking out a piece of paper.

WORKBOOK PAGE 11

A. LANGUAGES AND COUNTRIES

1. England, the United States, Australia, New Zealand, Canada
2. Argentina, Bolivia, Chile, Cuba, the Dominican Republic, Ecuador, etc.
3. Egypt, Jordan, Saudi Arabia
4. Portugal, Brazil

B. COUNTRY, NATIONALITY, OR LANGUAGE?

1. Arabic
2. Argentina
3. France
4. Taiwanese
5. Poland
6. Vietnamese
7. Honduras
8. Jordanian
9. Romanian
10. Japanese

C. WHAT'S THE WORD?

1. Italian
2. Portuguese
3. Poland
4. Turkish
5. Latvian
6. Korean
7. Spanish
8. English

WORKBOOK PAGE 12

A. MATCHING

1. f
2. c
3. a
4. e
5. d
6. b

B. LISTENING: *CALLING FOR A TAXI*

Listen to the conversation. Write the number next to the correct words.

1. A. City Taxi Company.
   B. Hello. Please send a taxi to 23 Elm Street.
   A. Is that a house or an apartment?
   B. It's a single-family house.
2. A. Hello. This is Yellow Taxi.
   B. Hello. Please send a taxi to 511 45th Street.
   A. Is that a house or apartment?
   B. It's a townhouse.
3. A. Good morning. This is Red Top Taxi.
   B. Good morning. Could you send a taxi to 3210 M Street?
   A. Okay. Is that a private home?
   B. No. It's a dormitory.
4. A. Diamond Taxi.
   B. Hello. We need a taxi at 34 Rose Court.
   A. Is there an apartment number?
   B. No. It's a mobile home.
5. A. Hello. Orange Cab. Can I help you?
   B. Yes. Please send a taxi to 4520 Lee Highway.
   A. Is that a house or an apartment?
   B. It's a nursing home.

Answers

3   2   4   5   1

C. CROSSWORD *(see p. 145)*

WORKBOOK PAGE 13

A. MAKING LISTS

List 3 things you can sit on:
armchair
soft/couch
loveseat

List 4 things you can plug in:
lamp   VCR
television   stereo system

B. WHERE IS IT?

1. television
2. lamp
3. drapes
4. photograph
5. pillow
6. plant
7. speaker

C. ANALOGIES

1. floor
2. fireplace
3. end table
4. wall unit
5. couch
6. video cassette recorder

WORKBOOK PAGE 14

A. MAKING LISTS

List 6 things on the table:	List 4 things on the buffet:	List 4 things on the serving cart:
candlestick	salad bowl	teapot
tablecloth	pitcher	coffee pot
centerpiece	serving bowl	creamer
salt shaker	serving platter	sugar bowl
pepper shaker		
butter dish		

B. MATCHING

1. f
2. a
3. e
4. c
5. d
6. b

C. MATCHING: *COMPOUND WORDS*

1. teapot
2. tablecloth
3. centerpiece
4. candlestick

D. WHICH WORD DOESN'T BELONG?

1. candle (The others hold liquids.)
2. sugar bowl (The others are furniture.)
3. chandelier (The others go on a table.)
4. tablecloth (The others hold food or liquid.)
5. serving bowl (The others are furniture.)
6. table (The others are for light.)

E. LISTENING: *WHAT DO THEY NEED?*

Listen to the conversation. Write the number next to the correct words.

1. A. Would you like a glass of water?
   B. Yes, thank you.
2. A. Would you like a cup of tea?
   B. Yes, thank you.
3. A. Would you care for a cup of coffee?
   B. Yes, thank you.
4. A. Could you pass the butter, please?
   B. Yes, of course.
5. A. Would you like sugar in your tea?
   B. Yes, please.

Answers

2   3   1   4   5

WORKBOOK PAGE 15

A. ON THE TABLE

1. wine glass
2. teaspoon
3. knife
4. napkin
5. butter knife
6. dinner fork
7. tablecloth
8. soup spoon

B. WHICH WORD?

1. fork
2. bowl
3. knife
4. glass
5. saucers
6. napkin

WORKBOOK PAGE 16

A. THINGS FOR THE BEDROOM

1. headboard
2. pillowcase
3. electric
4. alarm clock
5. mirror
6. jewelry box
7. clock radio
8. blinds

B. WHICH WORD DOESN'T BELONG?

1. cot (The others are bed coverings.)
2. blinds (The others are parts of a bed.)
3. clock radio (The others are bed coverings.)
4. mirror (The others are types of beds.)
5. king-size bed (The others are smaller beds.)
6. mirror (The others are bed coverings.)
7. jewelry box (The others are bed coverings.)

C. MAKE THE BED!

4
5
1
6
3
2

D. LISTENING: *WHAT IS IT?*

Listen to the conversation about beds. Write the number under the correct picture.

1. A. Excuse me. I'm looking for a trundle bed.
   B. We have some very nice trundle beds on sale this week.
2. A. Excuse me. Do you have any bunk beds?
   B. Yes. We have bunk beds right over here.
3. A. I'm looking for a sofa bed.
   B. What kind of sofa bed are you interested in?
4. A. Excuse me. We need a cot. Do you sell cots at this store?
   B. Yes, we do. Come right over here.
5. A. Do you have any twin beds on sale this week?
   B. Yes, we do.

Answers

3   2   5   4   1

WORKBOOK PAGE 17

A. WHERE ARE THEY?

1. placemats
2. cutting board
3. refrigerator magnet
4. paper towel holder
5. toaster
6. microwave (oven)
7. cookbook
8. (electric) can opener

B. MATCHING

1. c
2. d
3. g
4. a
5. f
6. b
7. e

C. MATCHING: *COMPOUND WORDS*

1. cookbook
2. potholder
3. placemat
4. dishwasher

D. CROSSWORD (see p. 146)

WORKBOOK PAGE 18

A. MAKING A LIST

pressure cooker	toaster oven	electric frying pan
coffeemaker	electric mixer	waffle iron
coffee grinder	food processor	electric griddle
popcorn maker	blender	

B. WHAT'S THE WORD?

1. coffee grinder
2. popcorn maker
3. bottle opener
4. can opener
5. egg beater
6. vegetable peeler

C. WHICH WORD?

1. food processor
2. garlic press
3. kettle
4. colander
5. bottle opener

D. MATCHING: *ASSOCIATIONS*

1. d
2. a
3. b
4. e
5. c

WORKBOOK PAGE 19

A. MATCHING: *ASSOCIATIONS*

1. b
2. d
3. c
4. e
5. a

B. WHICH WORD?

1.	cradle	5.	portable crib
2.	doll	6.	diaper pail
3.	high chair	7.	toy chest
4.	rattle	8.	baby carrier

C. WHICH WORD DOESN'T BELONG?

1. mobile (The others move a baby around)
2. crib (The others are toys.)
3. diaper pail (The others are furniture a baby can sit in.)
4. stretch suit (The others are items a baby can sit in.)
5. toy chest (The others are toys.)
6. intercom (The others are items a baby sits on.)

D. MATCHING

1.	c	6.	d
2.	j	7.	e
3.	h	8.	b
4.	a	9.	f
5.	i	10.	g

WORKBOOK PAGE 20

A. WHICH WORD?

1.	shampoo	6.	disposable
2.	vitamins	7.	cotton swabs
3.	teething ring	8.	bib
4.	pacifier	9.	teething ring
5.	formula	10.	nipple

B. LISTENING: *WHAT ARE THEY TALKING ABOUT?*
Listen to the conversation. Circle the correct words.

1. A. Excuse me. I can't find the liquid vitamins.
    B. We're out of liquid vitamins. We'll have them tomorrow.
2. A. Where did you put the teething ring?
    B. It's in the playpen.
3. A. I can't find the baby wipes. Where did you put them?
    B. The baby wipes are next to the changing table.
4. A. Where are disposable diapers? I can't find them.
    B. Disposable diapers are in the next aisle.
5. A. Excuse me. Where is baby formula?
    B. Sorry. We're out of formula, but we'll have more tomorrow.
6. A. Honey? Where did you put the pacifier?
    B. I thinks it's in the crib.

Answers

1.	liquid vitamins	4.	disposable diapers
2.	teething ring	5.	formula
3.	baby wipes	6.	pacifier

C. CROSSWORD (see p. 146)

WORKBOOK PAGE 21

A. WHERE ARE THEY?

1.	hamper	5.	toothbrush
2.	shelf	6.	plunger
3.	curtain	7.	cup
4.	mirror		

B. MATCHING

1.	e	6.	i
2.	d	7.	h
3.	a	8.	j
4.	c	9.	f
5.	b	10.	g

C. WHICH WORD?

1.	sponge	6.	fan
2.	hamper	7.	shower curtain
3.	soap	8.	seat
4.	rack	9.	scale
5.	toilet	10.	shower

D. THINGS IN THE BATHROOM

1.	fan	4.	shelf
2.	cup	5.	drain
3.	soap	6.	sink

WORKBOOK PAGE 22

A. MATCHING: *ASSOCIATIONS*

1.	c	4.	b
2.	a	5.	d
3.	f	6.	e

B. MATCHING: *HOW DO WE USE THEM?*

1.	c	4.	f
2.	a	5.	d
3.	b	6.	e

C. WHICH WORD DOESN'T BELONG?

1. mascara (The others are used for their scents.)
2. shower cap (The others are liquid hair care products.)
3. nail polish (The others are used in the hair.)
4. hairspray (The others are dental hygiene products.)
5. tweezers (The others are makeup.)
6. shoe polish (The others involve care of the fingernails.)

D. LISTENING: *WHAT ARE THEY TALKING ABOUT?*
Listen to the commercials. What products are they describing?
Check the correct answers.

1. Use it every day after you brush your teeth, and your teeth will be clean and healthy!
2. Your face will feel smooth all day!
3. Use it on shoes, boots, even pocketbooks! For a shine that lasts and lasts!
4. Keeps hair clean and shiny...smells nice, too!
5. Leaves lips shiny and moist...protects lips from the sun, too!
6. For that clean smell in every room of the house!
7. Put just a little blush on your cheeks for that healthy look!
8. Use the makeup base that looks perfect on you!
9. You'll smell fresh and clean all day!

Answers

1.	dental floss	4.	shampoo	7.	blush
2.	electric razor	5.	lipstick	8.	foundation
3.	shoe polish	6.	air freshener	9.	deodorant

WORKBOOK PAGE 23

A. WHAT ARE THEY?

1.	hanger	5.	dryer
2.	dustpan	6.	bleach
3.	recycling	7.	sponge
4.	iron	8.	clothespins

B. WHICH WORD?

1.	vacuum	5.	clothesline
2.	sponge mop	6.	bleach
3.	fabric softener	7.	hanger
4.	dryer	8.	garbage can

C. MATCHING

1.	d	5.	b
2.	e	6.	g
3.	a	7.	f
4.	h	8.	c

D. WHICH WORD DOESN'T BELONG?

1. hanger (The others are used for cleaning.)
2. sponge (The others hold things.)
3. starch (The others are appliances.)
4. floor wax (The others are containers.)
5. iron (The others are laundry powders or liquids.)
6. laundry bag (The others are used for cleaning.)

WORKBOOK PAGE 24

A. HOME REPAIRS
1. roof
2. antenna
3. satellite
4. lamppost
5. back
6. doorknob
7. screens
8. lawnmower
9. lawn chair
10. patio

B. MATCHING: *ASSOCIATIONS*
1. c
2. d
3. a
4. b
5. h
6. g
7. e
8. f

C. CROSSWORD (see p. 147)

WORKBOOK PAGE 25

A. MY APARTMENT BUILDING
1. doorman
2. intercom
3. mailboxes
4. elevator
5. chute
6. laundry
7. room
8. lot
9. swimming pool
10. lock
11. peephole
12. detector

B. MATCHING: *COMPOUND WORDS*
1. peephole
2. doorman
3. mailbox
4. whirlpool

C. WHICH WORD?
1. doorbell
2. buzzer
3. lot
4. fire alarm
5. garbage chute
6. storage room
7. air conditioner
8. peephole

WORKBOOK PAGES 26-27

A. REPAIR AND SERVICE PEOPLE
1. locksmith
2. plumber
3. gardener
4. carpenter
5. exterminator
6. painter

B. HELP!
1. exterminator
2. plumber
3. appliance repair person
4. electrician
5. gardener
6. chimney sweep
7. painter
8. handyman

C. MATCHING
1. e
2. b
3. a
4. f
5. d
6. c

D. WHAT KIND OF BILLS ARE THESE?
1. telephone bill
2. water bill
3. cable TV bill
4. electric bill
5. pest control bill
6. mortgage payment
7. gas bill
8. oil/heating bill

WORKBOOK PAGE 28

A. HOW ARE THEY USED?

...cut.	...paint.	...fasten things together.
hacksaw	paint pan	hammer
hatchet	paint roller	screwdriver
saw	paintbrush/brush	wrench
power saw	paint	pliers
	nail	

B. WHICH TOOLS?
1. hammer
2. bit
3. paint thinner
4. sandpaper
5. hatchet
6. paint
7. power saw
8. pliers

C. WHICH WORD DOESN'T BELONG?
1. toolbox (The others are tools.)
2. saw (The others are used for fastening.)
3. pliers (The others are used for painting.)
4. screw (The others are used for cutting.)
5. sandpaper (The others are tools.)
6. wire (The others are tools.)

D. LISTENING: *WHICH TOOL IS IT?*
Listen to the sounds. Write the number next to the tool you hear.
1. (Sound: electric drill)
2. (Sound: hammer)
3. (Sound: power saw)
4. (Sound: sandpaper)
5. (Sound: saw)
6. (Sound: scraper)
Answers
4   2   5   6   1   3

WORKBOOK PAGE 29

A. WHICH WORD?
1. mousetrap
2. plunger
3. yardstick
4. glue
5. vegetable seeds
6. flashlight
7. an extension cord
8. lawnmower
9. roach killer
10. fly swatter

B. MATCHING: *SENTENCES*
1. c
2. d
3. h
4. b
5. a
6. g
7. e
8. f

C. MATCHING
1. e
2. d
3. b
4. a
5. c
6. h
7. j
8. f
9. g
10. i

D. LISTENING: *WHAT ARE THEY TALKING ABOUT?*
Listen to the conversation. Circle the correct word.
1. A. Where are the work gloves?
   B. I lent them to the neighbors.
2. A. I can't find the trowel.
   B. I put the trowel in the tool shed.
3. A. Where's the plunger?
   B. In the bathroom.
4. A. I think we blew a fuse.
   B. I'll check it out.
5. A. Where did you put the step ladder?
   B. I don't remember!
6. A. We need oil.
   B. Okay. I'll get some at the hardware store.
7. A. Please get some fertilizer at the store.
   B. Okay. I'll get the kind that sprays from the hose.
8. A. We need insect spray.
   B. You're right. All these bugs are making me sick!
9. A. Can you help me move this wheelbarrow?
   B. Sure. I'll put it in the toolshed.
Answers
1. gloves
2. trowel
3. plunger
4. fuse
5. step ladder
6. oil
7. fertilizer
8. insect spray
9. wheelbarrow

WORKBOOK PAGE 30

A. MATCHING: *CARDINAL AND ORDINAL NUMBERS*

1. c		5. a	
2. g		6. b	
3. d		7. h	
4. f		8. e	

B. WHICH NUMBER?

1. fifteen		5. twentieth	
2. ninth		6. twenty-first	
3. third		7. fifty	
4. ten		8. first	

C. CROSSWORD: *NUMBERS TO WORDS* (see p. 147)

D. LISTENING: *WHAT'S THE NUMBER?*

Circle the correct number.

1. My youngest son is nine years old.
2. This is the fifth time I've been here.
3. We've been married for fourteen years.
4. My best friend lives on the eleventh floor of that apartment building.
5. There are eleven students in the class.
6. I bought this on sale for thirty-two dollars!
7. My uncle is fifty-five years old.
8. They're celebrating their thirteenth wedding anniversary.

Answers

1. nine		5. 11	
2. fifth		6. 32	
3. 14		7. 55	
4. 11th		8. 13th	

WORKBOOK PAGES 31-32

A. MATCHING: WORDS

1. c	3. d
2. a	4. b

B. MATCHING: *NUMBERS AND WORDS*

1. d	5. f
2. c	6. h
3. a	7. e
4. b	8. g

C. MATH SENTENCES

1. $3 \times 6 = 18$	3. $6 + 12 = 18$
2. $20 - 6 = 14$	4. $20 \div 2 = 10$

D. MATCHING: *WORDS AND FRACTIONS*

1. c	4. b
2. e	5. d
3. a	

E. WHAT FRACTION IS IT?

3/4   1/2   2/3   1/4   1/3

F. LISTENING: *WHAT'S THE FRACTION?*

Listen and write the number under the correct fraction.

1. One third of the class is absent today.
2. We'll leave in three quarters of an hour.
3. One fourth of the students in the class are from Europe.
4. The bicycle costs half the regular price.
5. The gas tank is about two thirds full.

Answers

4   2   5   1   3

G. MATCHING: *WORDS AND PERCENTS*

1. c	4. b
2. e	5. f
3. a	6. d

H. WHAT PERCENT IS IT?

100%   50%   75%   25%   66 2/3%

I. LISTENING: WHAT'S THE PERCENT?

Listen and write the number under the correct percent.

1. She got one hundred percent on the English test.
2. There's a sixty percent chance of snow tonight.
3. Twenty-five percent of the class has blue eyes.
4. The salesman took fifty percent off the regular price.
5. He got seventy-five percent of the answers right.

Answers

3   5   4   1   2

WORKBOOK PAGE 33

A. WHAT TIME IS IT?

1. 4:30	2. 4:00	3. 4:05
4. 4:15	5. 4:45	6. 4:40

B. MATCHING: *TIME*

1. 4:45, four forty-five
2. 5:30, five thirty
3. 5:40, twenty to six
4. 5:20, twenty after five
5. 5:50, ten to six

C. WHEN IS IT?

1. A.M.		3. midnight
2. noon		4. P.M.

D. LISTENING: *WHAT'S THE TIME?*

Listen and circle the correct time.

1. A. Excuse me. Could you tell me what time it is?
   B. Yes. It's three o'clock exactly.
2. A. What time will we arrive?
   B. At five ten a.m.
3. A. Excuse me. When does the train leave?
   B. At one oh five.
4. A. Excuse me. Do you have the time?
   B. Yes. It's five minutes after seven.
5. A. Excuse me. When will the train arrive?
   B. The train should arrive at about a quarter to four.
6. A. What time does the movie begin?
   B. At a quarter to eight.

Answers

1. 3:00		4. 7:05
2. 5:10		5. 3:45
3. 1:05		6. 7:45

WORKBOOK PAGE 34

B. USING THE CALENDAR

1. Thursday	4. Tuesday
2. Friday	5. Monday
3. Saturday	6. Wednesday

C. DATES: *WORDS TO NUMBERS*

1. 9/3/49	4. 2/12/95
2. 1/16/70	5. 11/10/76
3. 3/26/83	6. 12/12/12

D. DATES: *NUMBERS TO WORDS*

1. April 16, 1978	4. July 20, 1995
2. October 1, 1996	5. May 25, 1956
3. August 26, 1980	6. September 3, 1985

E. SEQUENCE

3	6	11	5
4	2	10	1
12	7	8	9

WORKBOOK PAGE 35

A. MAKING A LIST

bakery
cafeteria
donut shop
grocery store
coffee shop
convenience store
delicatessen/deli

B. WHICH PLACE?

1. barber shop
2. bakery
3. dry cleaners
4. pharmacy
5. furniture store
6. delicatessen
7. service station
8. donut shop
9. flower shop
10. concert hall

C. CROSSWORD: *PICTURES TO WORDS* (see p. 148)

WORKBOOK PAGE 36

A. GOING SHOPPING

1. mall
2. garage
3. music
4. pet
5. photo
6. toy
7. pizza
8. restaurant
9. theater

B. ANALOGIES

1. vision center
2. jewelry store
3. library
4. post office
5. travel agency
6. music store

C. MATCHING: *PLACES AND ACTIONS*

1. c
2. h
3. f
4. b
5. a
6. g
7. d
8. e

D. LISTENING: *WHERE ARE THEY?*

Listen to the conversation and circle the correct place.

1. A. Two tickets, please.
   B. For which movie?
   A. For "Home Alone 3."
2. A. We need a room for two nights.
   B. For how many people?
   A. For 2 adults and 2 children.
3. A. I'd like to look at engagement rings, please.
   B. Would you like to look at diamond rings?
   A. Yes, please.
4. A. We'd like to go to San Francisco.
   B. Do you want to fly first class?
   A. No. First class isn't necessary.
5. A. I'd like to try these shoes on.
   B. Fine. What size do you wear?
   A. I wear a 7 and a half.
6. A. I'd like to see a menu, please.
   B. Certainly. Would you like something to drink?
   A. Yes, please.
7. A. I'd like 2 slices of pizza, please.
   B. Is that to go or to eat here?
   A. I'll take it to go.
8. A. I'd like chocolate and vanilla, please.
   B. In a cone or a cup?
   A. In a cone.

Answers

1. movie theater
2. motel
3. jewelry store
4. travel agency
5. shoe store
6. restaurant
7. pizza shop
8. ice cream shop

WORKBOOK PAGE 37

A. WHERE IS IT?

1. bus
2. street
3. sidewalk
4. manhole
5. courthouse
6. subway station
7. fire station
8. intersection

B. MATCHING: *ASSOCIATIONS*

1. d
2. c
3. b
4. e
5. f
6. a

C. IN THE CITY

1. crosswalk
2. street sign
3. public telephone
4. newsstand
5. bank
6. taxi
7. intersection
8. meter maid

WORKBOOK PAGES 38-39

A. WHAT'S THE ANSWER?

1. long
2. bad
3. tall
4. loose
5. hot
6. single
7. wide
8. wet
9. dirty

B. ANTONYMS

1. young
2. new
3. heavy
4. dark
5. sharp
6. shiny
7. tall
8. long
9. easy
10. soft
11. curly
12. crooked

C. MY CAR

1. new
2. old
3. neat
4. fast
5. quiet
6. fancy
7. pretty
8. small
9. good
10. inexperience

D. CROSSWORD: *OPPOSITES* (see p. 148)

WORKBOOK PAGE 40

A. WHICH COLUMN?

happy emotions:	*sad* emotions:
proud	annoyed
ecstatic	miserable
pleased	disappointed
	frustrated

B. WHICH WORD?

1. cold
2. surprised
3. thirsty
4. sick
5. exhausted

C. MATCHING: *ASSOCIATIONS*

1. e
2. d
3. b
4. c
5. a

D. ANALOGIES

1. ecstatic
2. sick
3. cold
4. tired
5. unhappy

WORKBOOK PAGE 41

A. WHICH FRUIT DOESN'T BELONG?

1. lime
2. coconut
3. apricot
4. pineapple
5. strawberry

B. LISTENING: *WHAT FRUIT ARE THEY TALKING ABOUT?*
Circle the correct word.

1. A. I'm hungry. Do we have any fruit?
   B. Yes. We have apples.
2. A. Would you like a plum?
   B. Yes. Plums are delicious!
3. A. Where did you get the papaya?
   B. At the supermarket.
4. A. Do we have any more grapes?
   B. No. I'll get some tomorrow.
5. A. Would you like some watermelon?
   B. Yes, thank you.
6. A. Do we have any nectarines?
   B. No. I'll get some at the supermarket.
7. A. These cranberries are delicious!
   B. I like them, too.
8. A. Would you like a coconut?
   B. Yes, thank you.

Answers

1. apples
2. plums
3. papayas
4. grapes
5. watermelon
6. nectarines
7. cranberries
8. coconut

C. CROSSWORD: *PICTURES TO WORDS* (see p. 149)

(see p. 149)

WORKBOOK PAGE 42

A. WHICH GROUP?

1. lima bean
2. zucchini
3. yam
4. scallion

B. MATCHING

1. b
2. e
3. a
4. c
5. d

C. CROSSWORD: *PICTURES TO WORDS* (see p. 149)

(see p. 149)

WORKBOOK PAGES 43-44

A. WHICH GROUP?

Packaged Goods:	Beverages:	Canned Goods:	Dairy Products:
rice	diet soda	canned	milk
cereal	soda	vegetables	cheese
noodles	bottled water	soup	eggs
		tuna fish	

B. WHICH WORD?

1. milk
2. cream
3. cheese
4. fish
5. juice
6. juice
7. paks
8. soda

C. MORE GROUPS

Meat:	Poultry:	Seafood:	Baked Goods:
beef	chicken	salmon	bread
roast	duck	flounder	cake
lamb	turkey	shellfish	rolls

D. WHERE ARE THEY?

1. Poultry
2. Meat
3. Seafood
4. Baked Goods
5. Frozen Foods

E. MATCHING: *WHERE ARE THESE FOODS?*

1. e
2. b
3. d
4. a
5. c
6. h
7. i
8. f
9. j
10. g

F. WHAT'S THE WORD?

1. wings
2. trout
3. lemonade
4. mussels
5. steak
6. rolls

G. LISTENING: *WHAT ARE THEY TALKING ABOUT?*
Circle the correct word.

1. A. Let's have steak tonight.
   B. Good idea!
2. A. Excuse me. I'm looking for duck.
   B. It's in the Poultry Section.
3. A. Let's have lamb for dinner tonight.
   B. That sounds good!
4. A. I'm going to the supermarket.
   B. Get some ribs for dinner tonight, okay?
5. A. Pardon me. Where can I find haddock?
   B. In the Seafood Section.
6. A. Are you going to the supermarket? We need a roast.
   B. Okay. I'll get it.
7. A. How about shellfish tonight?
   B. Okay. Let's have oysters.
8. A. Do we need chicken from the supermarket?
   B. Yes. Get some legs, please.

Answers

1. steak
2. duck
3. lamb
4. ribs
5. haddock
6. roast
7. oysters
8. legs

WORKBOOK PAGE 45

A. WHICH GROUP?

1. mozzarella
2. pretzels
3. cole slaw
4. cocoa
5. bologna
6. relish

B. MATCHING

1. c
2. e
3. d
4. f
5. b
6. a

C. MATCHING: *ASSOCIATIONS*

1. c
2. d
3. b
4. f
5. a
6. e

D. WHICH WORD?

1. basket
2. towels
3. diapers
4. aisle
5. bag
6. coupons

E. LISTENING: *WHAT SECTION?*

Listen to the conversation and circle the correct section.

1. A. Do we need any of these paper plates?
   B. No, but we need paper cups.
2. A. Paper or plastic bag?
   B. Paper, please. And here are my coupons.
3. A. This formula is on sale.
   B. Good. We can get some wipes, too.
4. A. We need coffee, don't we?
   B. No, but I'd like to get some herbal tea.
5. A. I think I'll bake a cake this weekend.
   B. Do you need this cake mix?
6. A. Let's pick up some turkey and bologna.
   B. Okay. The potato salad looks good, too.
7. A. Pick up some salt and pepper.
   B. We could use some salad dressing, too.
8. A. Let's buy some chips for the party tonight.
   B. Great. How about some pretzels, too?

Answers

1. Paper Products
2. Checkout Area
3. Baby Products
4. Coffee and Tea
5. Baking Products
6. Deli
7. Condiments
8. Snack Foods

WORKBOOK PAGE 46

A. WHAT'S THE CONTAINER?

box   roll   bag
bunch   can   jar

B. WHAT'S THE WORD?

1. pound
2. head
3. bar
4. gallon
5. loaf
6. dozen
7. box
8. ear

C. WHICH WORD?

1. tub
2. packs
3. roll
4. half-gallon
5. pound
6. head

D. LISTENING: *WHAT ARE THEY TALKING ABOUT?*

Listen to the conversation and circle the correct words.

1. A. What did you get at the supermarket?
   B. I got two six-packs of soda and a bag of chips.
2. A. Do you have more than eight items?
   B. No. I only have a loaf of bread.
3. A. Could you please pick up a half-gallon of milk?
   B. A half-gallon? Certainly.
4. A. I bought a package of your favorite muffins.
   B. Thank you!
5. A. Would you pick up a bottle of ketchup at the supermarket?
   B. Sure. Is there anything else?
6. A. Would you like corn for dinner tonight?
   B. Yes. Let's get a few ears.
7. A. I'd like some ice cream for dessert tonight.
   B. Should I get a quart of vanilla or chocolate?
8. A. Let's get a couple of boxes of crackers for the party tonight.
   B. Okay. What kind do you like?

Answers

1. two six-packs
2. a loaf
3. a half-gallon
4. package
5. bottle
6. a few ears
7. quart
8. boxes

WORKBOOK PAGE 47

A. MATCHING: *ABBREVIATIONS*

1. d
2. a
3. c
4. e
5. b
6. h
7. i
8. j
9. f
10. g

B. WHICH IS EQUAL?

1. c
2. e
3. a
4. b
5. d

C. WHICH WORD?

1. tablespoons
2. 3/4 lb.
3. cups
4. teaspoon
5. gallon
6. cup

D. WHAT'S THE NUMBER?

1. 1
2. 2
3. 2
4. 64
5. 128
6. 1
7. 32
8. 2

E. LISTENING

Listen and circle the correct words.

1. A. How much flour should I put in?
   B. Add two cups.
2. A. These cookies are delicious! What did you put in them?
   B. A cup of nuts.
3. A. How much milk did you put in the scrambled eggs?
   B. One tablespoon.
4. A. How much ground beef would you like?
   B. I'd like a half a pound, please.
5. A. These cookies are salty! How much salt did you put in?
   B. Two tablespoons.
6. A. I'd like a quarter of a pound of turkey, please.
   B. Did you say a quarter?
7. A. How much cheese should I put in?
   B. The recipe says half an ounce.
8. A. Could you pick up a quart of milk?
   B. A quart? Okay.

Answers

1. two cups
2. a cup
3. a tablespoon
4. half a pound
5. two tablespoons
6. a quarter of a pound
7. half an ounce
8. quart

WORKBOOK PAGE 48

A. MATCHING

1. b
2. f
3. e
4. c
5. d
6. a

B. HELP IN THE KITCHEN

1. bake
2. beat
3. slice
4. pour
5. scrambling
6. stir-frying
7. barbecue
8. boil

C. SPELLING RULE

1. slicing
2. carving
3. scrambling
4. grating
5. baking
6. combining

WORKBOOK PAGE 49

A. ORDERING FAST FOOD

1. c
2. d
3. e
4. b
5. a

B. WHICH WORD DOESN'T BELONG?

1. taco (The others are beverages.)
2. BLT (The others are forms of bread.)
3. iced tea (The others are sandwiches.)
4. donut (The others are types of bread.)
5. chicken (The others are from beef.)
6. danish (The others are types of bread.)

C. LISTENING: *TAKING FAST FOOD ORDERS*

Listen to the order and put a check next to the correct item.

1. A. May I help you?
   B. Yes. I'll have a roast beef sandwich on white bread.
2. A. May I help you?
   B. Yes. I'll have a biscuit and a cup of coffee.
3. A. What would you like?
   B. I'd like a taco and a bowl of chili. Not too hot.
4. A. May I help you?
   B. Yes, thank you. Tuna fish on white.
5. A. Good afternoon. What can I get for you?
   B. Hello. I'll have a bacon, lettuce, and tomato sandwich. No mayonnaise.
6. A. May I help you?
   B. Yes. I'll have a chicken salad sandwich on rye.

Answers

1. roast beef
2. biscuit
3. taco
4. tuna fish
5. BLT
6. rye bread

WORKBOOK PAGES 50-51

A. ORDERING

1. shrimp cocktail
2. antipasto
3. veal cutlet
4. noodles
5. apple pie

B. LISTENING: *ORDERING AT A RESTAURANT*

You're a waiter or waitress. Listen to the order and check the correct items.

1. A. Good evening. May I take your order?
   B. Yes. For an appetizer I'll have the potato skins.
   A. And what kind of salad would you like?
   B. I'll have the spinach salad.
   A. And for the main course?
   B. I'd like the roast beef.
   A. What side dish would you like with that?
   B. I'll have the mixed vegetables.
   A. Would you care for dessert later?
   B. Yes. I think I'll have jello.

2. A. Hello. My name is John, and I'll be your waiter this evening. Are you ready to order?
   B. Yes. What do you recommend as an appetizer?
   A. The chicken wings are very good.
   B. Okay. I'll try them.
   A. What kind of salad do you care for today?
   B. Oh, just a tossed salad. No, wait a minute. I think I'll have a Greek salad.
   A. Okay. . . . And for an entree?
   B. How's the meatloaf?
   A. It's good. But the broiled fish is excellent.
   B. Okay I'll have the broiled fish. And can I have some rice with that?
   A. Certainly. And for dessert?
   B. I don't think I'll order dessert now. Maybe later.
   A. All right.

Answers

1. Appetizers: potato skins
   Salads: spinach salad
   Main Courses/Entrees: roast beef
   Side Dishes: mixed vegetables
   Desserts: jello

2. Appetizer: chicken wings
   Salads: Greek salad
   Main Courses/Entrees: broiled fish
   Side Dishes: rice
   Desserts: none

WORKBOOK PAGE 52

A. MATCHING: *ASSOCIATIONS*

1. c
2. a
3. e
4. f
5. d
6. b

B. WHICH COLOR?

1. gray
2. blue
3. green
4. red, white
5. Gold
6. black, white

WORKBOOK PAGE 53

A. WHICH WORD?

1. shirt
2. gown
3. sweater
4. jacket
5. suit
6. skirt

B. MATCHING: *COMPOUND WORDS*

1. jumpsuit
2. turtleneck
3. overalls
4. necktie

C. MAKING CLOTHES

1. tie
2. dress
3. jeans
4. coat
5. vest
6. gown
7. tights
8. jacket

D. CROSSWORD: *PICTURES TO WORDS* (see p. 150)

WORKBOOK PAGE 54

A. WHICH WORD?

1. pajamas
2. work boots
3. sneakers
4. slippers
5. sandals
6. long underwear
7. robe

B. WHICH WORD DOESN'T BELONG?

1. underpants (The others are shoes.)
2. stockings (The others are types of shoes.)
3. boots (The others are underwear.)
4. pajamas (The others are worn on the legs or feet.)
5. slip (The others are types of shoes.)
6. socks (The others are underwear.)

C. MATCHING

1. g
2. b
3. d
4. f
5. c
6. a
7. e

D. LISTENING: *WHAT ARE THEY TALKING ABOUT?*

Listen to the conversation and circle the correct word.

1. A. I can't find my brand new shorts.
   B. Did you look for them in the dresser?
2. A. I bought some new high tops today.
   B. They look nice.
3. A. Have you seen my new slippers?
   B. They're probably in the closet.
4. A. I got some new pumps, but I can't find them.
   B. Did you look under the bed?
5. A. I need to get some new pajamas.
   B. We can go shopping tonight.
6. A. Where are my new socks? Do you know?
   B. Hmm. Check in your bureau.

7. A. I'm looking for my nightshirt. Do you know where it is?
   B. Look in the wash.
8. A. New shoes?
   B. Yes. They arc.

Answers

1. shorts
2. high tops
3. slippers
4. pumps
5. pajamas
6. socks
7. nightshirt
8. shoes

WORKBOOK PAGE 55

A. WHICH GROUP?

jackets:	hats:	pants:
windbreaker	cap	tennis shorts
parka	beret	running shorts
down vest	rain hat	sweat pants

B. WHAT DO WE WEAR?

. . . when it's hot?	. . . when it's raining?	. . . when it's snowing?
tank top	rubbers	ear muffs
shorts	raincoat	ski jacket
sandals	poncho	mittens

C. MATCHING: *WHICH PART OF THE BODY?*

1. e
2. d
3. f
4. g
5. b
6. c
7. a

D. LISTENING: *WHAT ARE THEY TALKING ABOUT?*

Listen to the conversation and circle the correct word.

1. A. Is this hat yours?
   B. Yes. It's mine. Thanks.
2. A. What's the weather like?
   B. It's cool. Wear your overcoat.
3. A. I found these sweat pants.
   B. Thanks. They're mine.
4. A. I went shopping and got a new trenchcoat.
   B. Nice!
5. A. That's a nice beret you have on.
   B. Thank you.
6. A. It's cold outside today.
   B. Okay. I think I'll wear my parka.
7. A. It's going to be cold and snow all day today.
   B. I'll wear my ear muffs.
8. A. I found these tennis shorts in the dryer. Are they yours?
   B. Yes. They're mine. Thanks.

Answers

1. hat
2. overcoat
3. sweat pants
4. trenchcoat
5. beret
6. parka
7. ear muffs
8. tennis shorts

WORKBOOK PAGE 56

A. WHERE DO WE WEAR THEM?

neck:	finger:	wrist:	waist:
necklace	ring	bracelet	belt
beads	wedding band	watch	
chain			

B. MATCHING: *HOW DO WE USE THEM?*

1. d
2. e
3. b
4. h
5. a
6. g
7. f
8. c

C. MATCHING: *COMPOUND WORDS*

1. necklace
2. pocketbook
3. handbag
4. backpack
5. briefcase
6. earring

D. WHICH WORD DOESN'T BELONG?

1. wallet (The others are bags.)
2. key chain (The others are jewelry.)
3. key ring (The others are jewelry.)
4. bracelet (The others are bags.)
5. tote bag (The others are jewelry.)

WORKBOOK PAGE 57

A. WHAT'S THE WORD?

1. plain
2. low
3. wide
4. baggy
5. heavy
6. dark

B. WHAT'S THE WORD?

1. striped
2. narrow
3. baggy
4. long
5. light
6. small
7. narrow
8. long

C. LISTENING: *WHAT ARE THEY DESCRIBING?*

Listen to the conversation. Put the number next to the correct description.

1. How do you like this solid blue tie?
2. Are these plaid pants on sale?
3. I prefer the checked coat.
4. I really like that striped suit.
5. Your paisley scarf is so colorful!
6. I'm looking for a flowered skirt.
7. I prefer a simple print shirt.
8. How do you like the polka dot tie?

Answers

4	3	2	8
7	6	5	1

D. WHICH WORD DOESN'T BELONG?

1. tight
2. low
3. fancy
4. long
5. short
6. dark

WORKBOOK PAGE 58

A. MATCHING: *DEPARTMENTS*

1. e
2. a
3. b
4. c
5. g
6. d
7. h
8. f

B. WHICH WORD?

1. snack bar
2. directory
3. parking lot
4. customer pickup area
5. escalator
6. water fountain

C. LISTENING

Listen to the conversation. Write the number next to the correct place.

1. A. Excuse me. Are there any radios on sale?
   B. Yes, sir. They're over there, next to the tape recorders and clock radios.
2. A. What floor are you going to?
   B. The third floor. Could you push three for me, please?
3. A. I'll have a hot dog and a soda, please.
   B. Would you like a large or a small soda?
4. A. Try this. I think you'll like the smell.
   B. Hmm. "Sweet Scent". How much does a bottle of this cost?
5. A. My daughter usually wears a size 7 dress.
   B. Kids grow so fast. Maybe you should buy this dress in a size 8.
6. A. These earrings are lovely.
   B. Yes, they are. And we have a necklace that goes very well with them.

7. A. Which beds are on sale this week?
   B. The twin beds over there, next to the lamps.
8. A. Watch your step, Johnny. Put your hand on the railing.
   B. I like this better than the elevator, Mommy!
9. A. It's so hard to find a space!
   B. I see a man moving his car. Over there!

Answers

4	6
1	2
9	3
5	8
7	

WORKBOOK PAGE 59

A. ANOTHER WAY OF SAYING IT

1. compact disc
2. television
3. video cassette recorder
4. (personal) cassette player
5. video camera
6. sound system
7. boom box
8. cassette

B. MATCHING: *ASSOCIATIONS*

1. c
2. d
3. e
4. b
5. a

C. ANALOGIES

1. turntable
2. VCR
3. Walkman
4. audio cassette
5. videotape
6. headphones

D. MATCHING: *IDENTIFYING EQUIPMENT*

1. e
2. b
3. a
4. c
5. d

WORKBOOK PAGE 60

A. MATCHING: *WHAT EQUIPMENT DO YOU NEED?*

1. e
2. d
3. a
4. g
5. h
6. f
7. b
8. c

B. MATCHING

1. e
2. f
3. b
4. g
5. h
6. a
7. c
8. d

C. LISTENING: *USING A CHECKLIST*

Listen to the conversation. Check the equipment included.

1. A. I saw your ad in the newspaper. Is this the computer on sale?
   B. Yes, it is. It's on sale for one thousand one hundred dollars.
   A. Is the monitor included?
   B. Yes, it is.
   A. Is the disk drive included?
   B. Yes, it is. The monitor, the disk drive, the keyboard, and the mouse are all included.
   A. How about the printer?
   B. No, sir. The printer and modem are not included.
   A. And software?
   B. Software is extra, sir.

2. A. We're organizing our office and we need a reliable computer system.
   B. Yes, sir. Right over here is the best system we have. The complete system will cost two thousand five hundred dollars.
   A. And what does the system include?

B. This includes the basics: the monitor, the disk drive, the keyboard, and the mouse. It also includes the printer and a modem.
   A. And software?
   B. The computer system comes with data processing software.

3. A. Which camera is the best?
   B. This one here. It's on sale for 79 dollars.
   A. And what is included in the price?
   B. You get the camera, the camera case, the flash attachment, and one roll of film.

Answers

1. ✓ monitor
   ✓ disk drive
   ✓ keyboard
   ✓ mouse
   __ printer
   __ modem
   __ software

2. ✓ monitor
   ✓ disk drive
   ✓ keyboard
   ✓ mouse
   ✓ printer
   ✓ modem
   ✓ software

3. ✓ camera
   __ zoom lens
   ✓ camera case
   ✓ flash attachment
   __ tripod
   ✓ film

WORKBOOK PAGE 61

A. TOYS

Toys we use inside:	Toys we use outside:
train set	bicycle
video game system	pail and shovel
jigsaw puzzle	skateboard

B. MATCHING

1. e
2. a
3. b
4. c
5. d
6. i
7. h
8. f
9. j
10. g

C. WHAT'S THE WORD?

1. coloring book
2. rubber ball
3. tricycle
4. paint set
5. construction set
6. wading pool
7. doll house
8. stuffed animal

WORKBOOK PAGES 62-63

A. AMERICAN COINS

dime   silver dollar   nickel   quarter   half dollar   penny

B. MATCHING

1. fifty cents, half dollar
2. five cents, nickel
3. ten cents, dime
4. one dollar, silver dollar
5. twenty-five cents, quarter
6. one cent, penny

C. AMOUNTS

5¢	25¢	6¢	35¢	75¢
$.05	$.25	$.06	$.35	$.75

D. AMERICAN CURRENCY

$10.00 $5.00 $6.00 $30.00 $55.00

E. MAKING CHANGE

1. $4.00
2. $.15 or 15¢
3. $5.00
4. $10.00
5. $.05 or 5¢
6. $100.00

F. LISTENING: *HOW MUCH?*

Listen to the conversation. Circle the correct amount.

1. A. Do you have enough money to go to the movies?
   B. Yes. I have ten dollars.
2. A. How much does it cost?
   B. Two fifty.
3. A. Do you have any change?
   B. I only have a dollar.

4. A. How much money do you have?
   B. I have five one-dollar bills and two quarters.
5. A. How much is it?
   B. Fifty-one dollars.
6. A. Do you have enough money?
   B. Yes. It only costs twenty-five dollars and thirty cents.
7. A. What's the cost?
   B. Fourteen fifty.
8. A. Do you have any cash?
   B. Let's see. . . I have twelve dollars and ten cents exactly.

Answers
1. $10.00   5. $51.00
2. $2.50   6. $25.30
3. $1.00   7. $14.50
4. $5.50   8. $12.10

WORKBOOK PAGES 64-65

A. IN THE BANK
1. teller   5. traveler's checks
2. check   6. monthly statement
3. money order   7. deposit slip
4. checkbook   8. withdrawal slip

B. MATCHING
1. d   5. c
2. e   6. g
3. a   7. h
4. b   8. f

C. WHICH WORD DOESN'T BELONG?
1. automatic teller (The others are people.)
2. safe deposit box (The others are paper.)
3. ATM card (The others are paper.)
4. security guard (The others are printed items.)
5. loan application (The others relate to checking.)

D. WHAT ARE YOU DOING?
1. 2945 5879
   Account Number

   | Total Withdrawal | $150.00 |

2. 1094 3875
   Account Number

   | Total Withdrawal | $250.00 |

3. 595 40985
   Account Number

   | TOTAL | $650.50 |

4. 4378 349
   Account Number

   | TOTAL | $450.30 |

5. (check for $115.00)   6. (check for 36.85)

WORKBOOK PAGES 66-67

A. WHICH WORD DOESN'T BELONG?
1. earlobe (The others are part of the leg.)
2. nose (The others are part of the eye.)
3. tongue (The others relate to hair.)
4. hip (The others are parts of the head.)
5. elbow (The others are part of the leg.)
6. armpit (The others relate to the mouth.)

B. MATCHING: *ASSOCIATIONS*
1. c   4. b
2. a   5. f
3. e   6. d

C. MATCHING: *CLOTHING AND THE BODY*
1. e   4. f
2. b   5. c
3. d   6. a

D. WHICH WORD?
1. beard   5. forehead
2. shin   6. leg
3. hip   7. knee
4. chin   8. tongue

E. WHICH WORD DOESN'T BELONG?
1. bones (The others are internal.)
2. veins (The others are parts of the hand.)
3. toenail (The others relate to fingers.)
4. skin (The others are parts of the foot.)
5. knuckle (The others relate to the circulation of blood.)
6. palm (The others are internal.)
7. muscle (The others are joints.)

F. MATCHING: *ASSOCIATIONS*
1. f   5. g
2. e   6. c
3. d   7. b
4. a

G. MATCHING: *CLOTHING AND THE BODY*
1. e   4. b
2. a   5. c
3. d

H. WHICH WORD?
1. lungs   4. heart
2. fingernails   5. stomach
3. bones   6. throat

I. LISTENING: *WHAT IS IT?*
Circle the correct word.
1. Oh! My stomach hurts!
2. I'm concerned about my tooth.
3. I'm glad to hear that your calf is okay.
4. My doctor wants me to have some tests for my bladder.
5. What's the matter with your skin?
6. My nose hurts!
7. My doctor is concerned about my hip.
8. I want to have some tests for my elbow.

Answers
1. stomach   5. skin
2. tooth   6. nose
3. calf   7. hip
4. bladder   8. elbow

WORKBOOK PAGES 68-69

A. MATCHING
1. i   6. h
2. f   7. e
3. a   8. g
4. c   9. j
5. b   10. d

B. WHAT'S THE MATTER?
1. stomachache   6. backache
2. sunburn   7. diarrhea
3. stiff neck   8. virus
4. chills   9. rash
5. cavity   10. sore throat

D. FEELING TERRIBLE
1. sprain   6. swollen
2. vomit   7. exhausted
3. itchy   8. burp
4. congested   9. bleeding
5. dislocate   10. coughing

E. CROSSWORD (see p. 150)

WORKBOOK PAGE 70

A. MATCHING: *WHAT DO THEY DO?*
1. h   6. d
2. e   7. b
3. a   8. j
4. g   9. c
5. i   10. f

B. WHAT WILL THEY USE?

1. Novocaine
2. thermometer
3. blood pressure gauge
4. X-ray machine
5. stethoscope
6. examination table
7. eye chart
8. scale

C. LISTENING: *WHO'S TALKING?*

Listen to the sentences. Circle the correct answer.

1. Your blood pressure is 90 over 60. That's good!
2. Your teeth are very clean now.
3. How do these glasses fit?
4. A good check-up! You don't have any cavities.
5. Congratulations! You're going to be a mother!
6. I'm going to look into your ears. This won't hurt at all!
7. You have a strong healthy heart.
8. I'm going to have to operate.
9. Please step over here to the X-ray machine.
10. Have a seat. What seems to be the problem?

Answers

1. nurse
2. hygienist
3. optometrist
4. dentist
5. obstetrician
6. pediatrician
7. cardiologist
8. surgeon
9. X-ray technician
10. psychiatrist

WORKBOOK PAGE 71

A. WHAT DID THE DOCTOR DO?

1. cast, sling
2. diet, exercise
3. prescription, rest
4. X-ray, crutches
5. stitches, bandaid

B. MATCHING: *WHAT DO THEY DO?*

1. d
2. a
3. b
4. e
5. c

C. WHICH WORD?

1. gown
2. diet
3. a prescription
4. control
5. physical therapy
6. pan
7. medical chart
8. I.V.
9. fluids
10. shot

WORKBOOK PAGE 72

A. SOLUTIONS

1. lozenge
2. cough
3. vitamins
4. aspirins
5. ointment
6. antacid
7. decongestant spray
8. ointment
9. creme
10. aspirin

B. WHAT'S THE MEDICINE?

1. b
2. a
3. a
4. a
5. b
6. b
7. a

C. LISTENING: *WHAT'S THE DOSAGE?*

Listen to the directions. Circle the correct answer.

1. The doctor told me to take 3 teaspoons every 6 hours.
2. Every morning I take one tablet after breakfast.
3. She told me to take 2 teaspoons after every meal.
4. The dosage is 2 caplets every six hours.
5. You will take a tablet every day.
6. Take one capsule, every six hours.
7. The doctor said to take five capsules.
8. He told me to take seven caplets every night before bed.

Answers

1. 3 teaspoons
2. 1 tablet
3. 2 teaspoons
4. 2 caplets
5. 1 tablet
6. 1 capsule
7. 5 capsules
8. 7 caplets

WORKBOOK PAGE 73

A. SENDING MAIL

1. parcel
2. parcel post
3. of stamps
4. postcard
5. letter
6. postage
7. letter
8. post
9. envelope
10. machine
11. bag
12. change-of-address

B. WHICH WORD DOESN'T BELONG?

1. window (The others appear on an envelope.)
2. mail truck (The others are people.)
3. mail bag (The others are classes of mail service.)
4. mail slot (The others are things to mail.)
5. scale (The others are things to mail.)
6. money order (The others are classes of mail service.)
7. postal clerk (The others appear on an envelope.)
8. express mail (The others are postal service property.)

C. MATCHING

1. registered mail
2. return address
3. third class
4. book rate
5. mail carrier
6. zip code

WORKBOOK PAGE 74

A. AT THE LIBRARY

1. librarian
2. card catalog
3. author
4. title
5. call number
6. shelves
7. magazines
8. periodicals
9. microfilm
10. library card
11. assistant
12. checkout desk

B. MATCHING: *LIBRARY HELP*

1. e
2. f
3. g
4. a
5. d
6. c
7. b

C. READING CALL CARDS

1. John A. Reynolds
2. 495
3. *Sports Around the World*
4. Sports
5. 295
6. 1991
7. *The Importance of English*
8. *American Short Stories*

WORKBOOK PAGE 75

A. AT SCHOOL

1. guidance counselor
2. teachers' lounge
3. cafeteria
4. locker
5. language lab
6. nurse
7. chemistry lab
8. track
9. teachers' lounge
10. field

B. MATCHING: *ASSOCIATIONS*

1. f
2. e
3. a
4. b
5. c
6. h
7. d
8. g

C. LISTENING: *WHO ARE THESE STUDENTS GOING TO SEE?*

Circle the correct word.

1. Attention, students. Sorry for the interruption. Would Jack Riley please report to the guidance counselor? Jack Riley—please report to the guidance counselor.
2. Please excuse the interruption. Would Cindy Bowman and Shirley Cross please meet Mr. Taylor for driver's education in the front parking lot?

3. Attention, all students and teachers. Mary Holmes and Janet Reed—please stop by the principal's office after school. Mary Holmes and Janet Reed to the principal's office after school. Thank you.
4. Attention, please. Sorry for the interruption. Johnny Brown. Johnny Brown. Please see Mrs. Wright for your eye examination.
5. Attention all students. All students willing to help clean the school grounds, report to Mr. Jackson in the basement after school. Thank you.
6. May I have your attention, please? George Walker—report to the cafeteria immediately.
7. Attention, please. All students interested in playing baseball, please meet in the gymnasium after school.
8. May I have your attention? Sorry for the interruption. Would Maria Jones please report to the office as soon as possible? Thank you.

Answers
1. guidance counselor
2. driver's ed instructor
3. principal
4. school nurse
5. custodian
6. lunchroom monitor
7. coach
8. assistant principal

WORKBOOK PAGES 76-77

A. WHERE DO THESE SUBJECTS BELONG?

Mathematics:	Sciences:	Languages:
algebra	biology	Spanish
geometry	physics	English
calculus	chemistry	French
trigonometry		

B. MATCHING: *ASSOCIATIONS*
1. e
2. a
3. d
4. g
5. f
6. b
7. c

C. MATCHING: *EXTRACURRICULAR ACTIVITIES*
1. g
2. e
3. f
4. c
5. b
6. a
7. d

D. LISTENING: *WHAT ARE THEY TALKING ABOUT?*
Listen to the sentences and circle the correct words.
1. I'm not going to practice today. I have a sore throat. I can't sing!
2. We're having a meeting after school tomorrow. Bring the articles you wrote.
3. The test was easy! I understand angles very well.
4. I can drive well, but I have trouble parking!
5. Vamos a estudiar para al examen.
6. Six points! What a touchdown!
7. That was lovely. You played very well.
8. I like to learn about the past!

Answers
1. choir
2. school newspaper
3. geometry
4. driver's ed
5. Spanish
6. football
7. band
8. history

E. CROSSWORD (see p. 151)

WORKBOOK PAGES 78-79

A. WHAT'S THE WORD?
1. cashier
2. baker
3. actress
4. carpenter
5. architect
6. assembler
7. artist
8. bricklayer
9. bookkeeper
10. chef

B. MATCHING: *WHAT DO THEY DO?*
1. f
2. e
3. i
4. j
5. a
6. g
7. h
8. b
9. c
10. d

C. WHICH GROUP?

These people cut hair:	These people cook:
barber	chef
hairdresser	baker

These people clean:	These people deliver:
custodian	courier
janitor	delivery person
housekeeper	messenger

These people work with numbers and money:	These people build:
accountant	mason
bookkeeper	bricklayer
cashier	

D. MATCHING: *COMPOUND WORDS*
1. housekeeper
2. bookkeeper
3. bricklayer
4. firefighter
5. hairdresser

E. LISTENING: *WHAT'S THE JOB?*
Listen and circle the correct word.
1. I meet a lot of people every day. I know the streets of the city well.
2. Every day I cut beef, chicken, veal, and pork for my customers.
3. I like to write and do research. I use a word processor.
4. People call me when there's an emergency.
5. I cut people's hair every day.
6. I work outside. My job can be dangerous, so I often wear a helmet to protect my head.
7. I build things with wood. I use a hammer and nails.
8. I'm very good in math. I like to work with numbers.

Answers
1. bus driver
2. butcher
3. journalist
4. firefighter
5. barber
6. construction worker
7. carpenter
8. bookkeeper

F. CAREER EXPLORATION
1. accountant, bookkeeper
2. artist, assembler
3. bricklayer, construction worker, farmer, gardener
4. artist, architect, chef/cook
5. fisherman, delivery person, courier/messenger
6. actor/actress, barber, hairdresser, cashier

WORKBOOK PAGES 80-81

A. JOBS
1. mechanic
2. plumber
3. real estate agent
4. pharmacist
5. receptionist
6. photographer
7. newscaster
8. pilot
9. sanitation worker
10. police officer

B. MATCHING: *WHERE DO THEY WORK?*
1. d
2. f
3. a
4. b
5. g
6. c
7. e

C. MATCHING: *ASSOCIATIONS*

1. b
2. c
3. a
4. e
5. d
6. j
7. i
8. f
9. g
10. h

D. WHAT'S THE WORD?

1. painter
2. interpreter
3. gardener
4. reporter
5. farmer
6. truck driver
7. photographer
8. waiter
9. welder

E. CROSSWORD (see p. 151)

WORKBOOK PAGES 82-83

A. MATCHING: *WHAT DO THEY DO?*

1. e
2. f
3. b
4. a
5. g
6. c
7. d
8. j
9. k
10. i
11. h
12. n
13. m
14. l

B. WHAT DO THEY DO?

1. paint
2. fix things
3. play an instrument
4. serve food
5. sew
6. teach
7. translate
8. type

C. WHAT'S THE WORK ACTIVITY?

draw   type   bake   assemble   grow

D. MATCHING: *ASSOCIATIONS*

1. e
2. d
3. b
4. c
5. f
6. a
7. h
8. i
9. l
10. k
11. g
12. j

E. MATCHING: *WHAT DOES IT MEAN?*

1. d
2. e
3. a
4. b
5. c

F. LISTENING: *WHAT DO THEY DO?*

Listen and put a check next to the correct sentence.

1. I'm a security guard. I usually work at night.
2. I'm an assembler at a factory.
3. I grow vegetables and fruits and raise animals.
4. I play an instrument in a musical group. I work with other musicians.
5. I'm an architect.
6. I work as an English professor at a university.
7. I'm a secretary in an office.
8. I'm a seamstress. I make suits for men and women.
9. I'm a construction worker.

Answers

1. I guard buildings.
2. I assemble components.
3. I'm a farmer.
4. I play the piano.
5. I design buildings.
6. I teach.
7. I type.
8. I sew.
9. I build things.

WORKBOOK PAGE 84

A. JOE'S DAILY ROUTINE

1. coat closet
2. mailbox
3. waste receptacle
4. message board
5. coffee machine
6. workstation
7. typist

B. WHICH WORD?

1. employee lounge
2. boss
3. supply
4. mailbox
5. office manager
6. office
7. storage room
8. workstations
9. reception area

C. MATCHING: *WHERE IS THIS CONVERSATION TAKING PLACE?*

1. e
2. c
3. d
4. b
5. a

D. LISTENING: *WHO IS TALKING?*

Listen and circle the correct answer.

1. I filed all the reports.
2. Good afternoon. Have a seat. I'll tell Mr. Brown you're here.
3. My typewriter is broken.
4. Paychecks will be ready at 12 noon.
5. You're hired! When can you start working?
6. The boss isn't here right now. Can I take a message?

Answers

1. file clerk
2. receptionist
3. typist
4. administrative assistant
5. boss
6. secretary

WORKBOOK PAGE 85

A. WHAT'S THE WORD?

1. calculator
2. microcassette recorder
3. fax machine
4. plastic binding machine
5. phone system
6. paper shredder

B. WHICH WORD?

1. printer
2. processor
3. shredder
4. system
5. scale
6. cutter

C. MATCHING: *ASSOCIATIONS*

1. e
2. d
3. b
4. c
5. a

D. LISTENING: *SOUND EFFECTS*

Listen to the sounds of office equipment. Write the number of the sound on the correct line.

1. telephone
2. electric pencil sharpener
3. adding machine
4. typewriter
5. fax machine
6. dot-matrix-printer

Answers

2   5   3
4   1   6

WORKBOOK PAGE 86

A. WHICH GROUP?

Types of chairs:	Things we write with:	Things we write in or on:
clerical	highlighter	organizer
posture	mechanical pencil	appointment book
swivel		timesheet

B. MATCHING: *ASSOCIATIONS*

1. b
2. g
3. h
4. a
5. c
6. e
7. d
8. f

C. ANALOGIES

1. typewriter
2. pencils
3. highlighter pen
4. staple remover
5. stamp pad

D. WHICH WORD?

1. pencil
2. calendar
3. book
4. opener
5. cabinet
6. tray
7. dispenser
8. ink

WORKBOOK PAGE 87

A. WHICH WORD?

1. correction fluid
2. paper clip
3. note pad
4. mailing label
5. carbon paper
6. paper fasteners
7. rubber cement
8. stationery
9. mailing label
10. manila folder

B. WHICH WORD?

1. legal
2. plastic
3. computer
4. Post-It note
5. sealing
6. typing

C. MATCHING: *WHAT DO WE USE IT FOR?*

1. d
2. g
3. f
4. e
5. a
6. b
7. h
8. i
9. c

WORKBOOK PAGE 88

D. LISTENING: *TAKING A MESSAGE*

Listen to the telephone conversations. Write the messages.

1. A. Could I speak to Mr. Taylor, please?
   B. Mr. Taylor isn't here right now. Would you like to leave a message?
   A. Yes, thank you. This is Mrs. Perez. Could you ask him to call me at (212) 986-3098?
   B. Certainly. That's (212) 986-3098.
   A. That's correct. And my name is Mrs. Perez. P-E-R-E-Z. Please ask him to call back today.
   B. All right. I'll give him the message.

2. A. This is Mr. White. I'd like to speak to Mr. Franco.
   B. Mr. Franco isn't here right now. Would you like to leave a message?
   A. Yes, thank you. Could you have him call me at (717) 554-8984?
   B. Yes. That's Mr. White at (717) 554-8984, right?
   A. Yes. And please tell him to call before 5:00.

3. A. May I speak to Mrs. Donna Ling? This is her husband, Mr. Ling.
   B. Mrs. Ling isn't here right now. Would you like to leave a message?
   A. Yes, please. She needs to call me immediately at (419) 354-3963.
   B. Is this urgent?
   A. Yes, it is.
   B. All right. And the number again is (419) 354-3963. Is that correct?
   A. Yes. That's correct. Thank you.

4. A. I'm returning Ms. Benson's phone call. This is Mrs. Hobbs.
   B. Ms. Benson isn't here right now. Could I take a message?
   A. No, that's okay. I'll call again. Just tell her I have some important news.
   B. All right

Answers

1.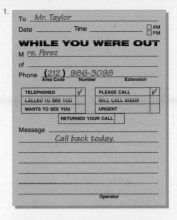

To Mr. Taylor
Date _____ Time _____ ☐ AM ☐ PM
WHILE YOU WERE OUT
M rs. Perez
of _____
Phone (212) 986-3098
Area Code Number Extension
TELEPHONED ✔ | PLEASE CALL ✔
CALLED TO SEE YOU | WILL CALL AGAIN
WANTS TO SEE YOU | URGENT
RETURNED YOUR CALL
Message
Call back today.
Operator

2.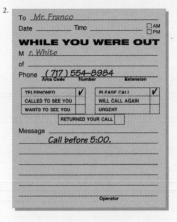

To Mr. Franco
Date _____ Time _____ ☐ AM ☐ PM
WHILE YOU WERE OUT
M r. White
of _____
Phone (717) 554-8984
Area Code Number Extension
TELEPHONED ✔ | PLEASE CALL ✔
CALLED TO SEE YOU | WILL CALL AGAIN
WANTS TO SEE YOU | URGENT
RETURNED YOUR CALL
Message
Call before 5:00.
Operator

3.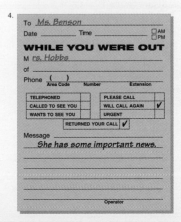

To Mrs. Ling
Date _____ Time _____ ☐ AM ☐ PM
WHILE YOU WERE OUT
M r. Ling
of _____
Phone (419) 354-3963
Area Code Number Extension
TELEPHONED ✔ | PLEASE CALL ✔
CALLED TO SEE YOU | WILL CALL AGAIN
WANTS TO SEE YOU | URGENT ✔
RETURNED YOUR CALL
Message
Call immediately.
Operator

4.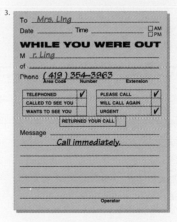

To Ms. Benson
Date _____ Time _____ ☐ AM ☐ PM
WHILE YOU WERE OUT
M rs. Hobbs
of _____
Phone ( )
Area Code Number Extension
TELEPHONED | PLEASE CALL
CALLED TO SEE YOU | WILL CALL AGAIN ✔
WANTS TO SEE YOU | URGENT
RETURNED YOUR CALL ✔
Message
She has some important news.
Operator

WORKBOOK PAGE 89

A. WHICH WORD?

1. fire extinguisher
2. vending machine
3. forklift
4. first-aid kit
5. payroll office
6. supply room
7. personnel office
8. foreman
9. card
10. suggestion box

B. MATCHING: *FINISH THE WORDS*

1. c
2. e
3. b
4. a
5. d
6. i
7. h
8. j
9. g
10. f

C. WHICH WORD?

1. machine
2. elevator
3. department
4. dock
5. office

D. MATCHING: *DEFINITIONS*

1. c
2. d
3. f
4. a
5. e
6. g
7. b

WORKBOOK PAGE 90

A. WHICH GROUP?

Vehicles:	Tools:	Building materials:
bulldozer	pickax	brick
pickup truck	shovel	cement
crane	jackhammer	plywood
van	sledgehammer	lumber

B. WHICH WORD?

1. wheelbarrow
2. helmet
3. plywood
4. trowel
5. blueprints
6. ladder
7. shingles
8. bulldozer

C. MATCHING: *COMPOUND WORDS*

1. backhoe
2. blueprints
3. bulldozer
4. pickax
5. sledgehammer
6. toolbelt
7. wheelbarrow

D. LISTENING: *WHAT ARE THEY TALKING ABOUT?*

Listen and circle the correct word.

1. The construction workers will bring the beam in the pickup truck.
2. Could you get me that trowel?
3. Let me show you how to start the van.
4. We need the blueprints as soon as possible.
5. Watch out for that backhoe!
6. They should use a level there.
7. Take the girder over there.
8. Can you pick up that shingle and bring it here?
9. Do you know how to operate a front-end loader?
10. Could I borrow your tape measure?
11. I can't find the hardhats!
12. I'll get more wire from the supply room.

Answers

1. beam
2. trowel
3. van
4. blueprints
5. backhoe
6. level
7. girder
8. shingle
9. front-end loader
10. tape measure
11. hardhats
12. wire

WORKBOOK PAGE 91

A. MATCHING: *WHAT SHOULD THEY USE?*

1. h
2. g
3. a
4. e
5. c
6. d
7. b
8. f

B. MATCHING: *COMPOUND WORDS*

1. tailpipe
2. headlight
3. hubcap
4. sunroof
5. dashboard
6. dipstick
7. windshield

C. WHICH WORD?

1. signal
2. mirror
3. plate
4. belt
5. tire
6. wipers
7. dipstick
8. seat belt

D. WHICH WORD?

1. visor
2. horn
3. ignition
4. stickshift
5. glove compartment
6. tow truck

E. MATCHING: *ASSOCIATIONS*

1. d
2. c
3. b
4. a
5. f
6. h
7. e
8. g
9. j
10. i

F. SAFETY FIRST

1. trunk
2. jumper cables
3. flares
4. jack
5. spare tire
6. seat belts
7. air bags

G. LISTENING: *CHECKLIST*

Listen to the car dealers. Put a check next to the item each car has.

1. A. This is a very nice car.
    B. I like the sunroof. Does this car come with a luggage carrier?
    A. No, it doesn't. But it has a very large trunk.
    B. I'd like to look in the truck. Oh, good. . . There's a jack and a spare tire, of course. I notice there isn't a side mirror.
    A. A side mirror is extra on this car. I can get one for you for about $100. Did I tell you about the cruise control?
    B. Yes, you did.
    A. And the rear defroster?
    B. Yes, you did. Does this car have an air bag?
    A. No, it doesn't. But it has a nice tape deck.

2. A. I'm interested in this car.
    B. Yes, ma'am. Now please understand. This car is our cheapest model. It doesn't have a lot of features. It doesn't have a sunroof or a luggage carrier.
    A. I understand. Is there a jack and a spare tire?
    B. Yes, of course. But there isn't a side mirror or cruise control.
    A. Rear defroster?
    B. Yes, ma'am. There is a rear defroster.
    A. Air bag?
    B. I'm afraid not in this model.
    A. Is there a tape deck?
    B. No, ma'am. There's a radio, but we can install a tape deck, if you want.

Answers

✔ sunroof	__ sunroof
__ luggage carrier	__ luggage carrier
✔ jack	✔ jack
✔ spare tire	✔ spare tire
__ side mirror	__ side mirror
✔ cruise control	__ cruise control
✔ rear defroster	✔ rear defroster
__ air bag	__ air bag
✔ tape deck	__ tape deck

WORKBOOK PAGE 93

A. WHICH WORD?

1. stop
2. exit
3. intersection
4. speed limit
5. crosswalk
6. service area
7. tollbooth
8. corner

B. MATCHING: *ASSOCIATIONS*

1. f
2. a
3. e
4. d
5. c
6. b

C. WHAT ARE THEY TALKING ABOUT?

1. school crossing
2. service area
3. yield sign
4. tollbooth
5. speed limit sign
6. tunnel

E. LISTENING: *TRAFFIC SIGNS*

Listen to the conversations. Write the number under the correct sign.

1. Careful! You can't make a left turn here!
2. Oh, you can't go there. It says, "Do not enter."
3. Didn't you see that sign? You were supposed to stop.
4. See that sign? You can't turn here.
5. You can't turn right here.

Answers

2   4   1   3   5

WORKBOOK PAGE 94

A. WHERE DID THEY GO?

1. train station
2. information booth
3. timetable
4. train
5. ticket window
6. arrival and departure board
7. track
8. porter
9. luggage
10. platform

B. WHICH WORD DOESN'T BELONG?

1. turnstile (The others are people.)
2. token (The others are people.)
3. sleeper (The others are used to pay a fare.)
4. engine (The others are places passengers wait.)
5. porter (The others are types of rail cars.)
6. transfer (The others are people.)

C. WHICH WORD?

1. sleeper
2. fare
3. platform
4. bus station
5. timetable
6. token
7. redcap
8. counter

D. WHERE ARE THEY?

Listen to the conversations and decide where the passengers are.

1. Can I please have a transfer?
2. Buy your token. Then put it in the turnstile.
3. Can you recommend a hotel near here?
4. The porter is taking your luggage to your sleeper.
5. The food smells good!
6. The meter says you own me 15 dollars, sir.

Answers

4	2	5
6	1	3

WORKBOOK PAGE 95

A. WHICH WORD?

1. check-in counter
2. suitcase
3. metal detector
4. boarding pass
5. waiting area
6. skycap
7. declaration form
8. garment bag

B. WHICH WORD DOESN'T BELONG?

1. luggage carrier (The others are people.)
2. immigration (The others refer to baggage.)
3. X-ray machine (The others are paper.)
4. baggage carousel (The others relate to security.)
5. immigration (The others are in passenger waiting areas.)
6. gate (The others are documents.)

C. A TICKET

1. James Johnson
2. United Airlines
3. July 5
4. 5:05 P.M.
5. Chicago
6. Madrid
7. 723
8. $804.00
9. May 12

WORKBOOK PAGE 96

A. WHAT DO THEY NEED?

1. air sickness bag
2. seat control
3. lavatory
4. overhead compartment
5. oxygen mask
6. galley

B. WHICH WORD?

1. panel
2. belt
3. exit
4. building
5. gear
6. nose

C. MATCHING: *WHAT IS IT?*

1. d
2. f
3. e
4. a
5. g
6. c
7. h
8. b

D. LISTENING

Listen and check the words you hear.

1. Good morning, ladies and gentlemen and welcome to flight 304 to San Francisco. This is your flight attendant, Sally. Let me go over a few safety suggestions. In case of an emergency, the oxygen mask will appear from above your seat. Pull the mask over your nose and mouth and breathe normally. Please take a minute to look at the emergency instruction card located in the seat pocket in front of you. You will find emergency exits on both sides of the cabin. Now, if you will fasten your seat belt, we are about to take off. We will begin serving your meal about 30 minutes after takeoff.
2. Good evening, passengers. This is your co-pilot, Captain Jack Martino. Welcome to Flight 734 to New York City. You'll notice the Fasten Seat Belt sign is on. We'll be on the runway for about 3 minutes, and then we'll take off. On behalf of your pilot and flight attendants, I hope you enjoy this evening's flight.
3. Ladies and gentlemen, we'll be landing at London's Heathrow Airport in about 15 minutes. Please fasten your seat belts and observe the No Smoking sign. Please put your trays up and put any bags under the seat in front of you. Please remain in your seats until the airplane taxis to the terminal building and comes to a complete stop.

Answers

1. ✓ seat belt
   __ bathroom
   __ life vest
   __ call button
   ✓ oxygen mask
   ✓ emergency exit
   ✓ meal
   ✓ emergency
      instruction card

2. ✓ co-pilot
   __ flight engineer
   ✓ flight attendants
   __ window seat
   ✓ Fasten Seat Belt sign
   __ meal
   ✓ runway
   __ control tower

3. ✓ tray
   __ oxygen mask
   ✓ seat belt
   __ seat control
   __ landing gear
   __ runway
   ✓ terminal building
   ✓ No Smoking sign

WORKBOOK PAGE 97

A. WHAT'S THE WORD?

1. raining
2. foggy
3. snowing
4. clear
5. windy

B. MATCHING: *ASSOCIATIONS*

1. c
2. a
3. d
4. b
5. g
6. e
7. h
8. f

C. FAHRENHEIT AND CELSIUS

1. a
2. b
3. a
4. a
5. b
6. a

D. LISTENING: *WEATHER FORECASTS*

Listen and write the number under the correct picture.

1. Good morning. It's going to be hot and muggy today. In fact, it will reach 90 degrees Fahrenheit by this afternoon. It will cool off this evening with an eighty percent chance of a thunderstorm.
2. Tomorrow's forecast looks like this: We can expect that snowstorm to arrive early in the morning. Snow will accumulate two to four inches. Temperatures will drop to 25 degrees Fahrenheit.
3. The forecast for the next few days looks like this: cool in the mornings, but warm, sunny afternoons. An April drizzle will help those buds blossom into flowers.
4. For the next few days, we'll have warm sunny days and cool, clear evenings—perfect weather to watch the leaves turn color!

Answers

1   4   3   2

WORKBOOK PAGE 98

A. WHICH WORD?

1. bag
2. basket
3. stakes
4. trail map
5. lantern
6. thermos
7. backpack
8. rope

B. MATCHING

1. b
2. d
3. a
4. c
5. g
6. h
7. f
8. e

C. MATCHING

1. d
2. c
3. f
4. e
5. b
6. a

D. LISTENING: *WHERE ARE THEY GOING?*

Listen and write the number next to the correct word.

1. A. Great idea! Let's go this weekend!
   B. I have one problem. I don't have a harness.
   A. That's not a problem. I have a rope and harness you can use.
2. A. Let's go under those trees!
   B. But there isn't a table.
   A. That's okay. I brought a blanket to sit on.
   B. Okay. Let's see what's in the basket. I'm hungry!
3. A. Which way do we go now?
   B. I don't know. Let's look at the trail map.
4. A. Here are the sleeping bags. Where is the tent? In your backpack?
   B. No. Let's sleep under the stars tonight!

Answers

4   3   1   2

WORKBOOK PAGE 99

A. WHICH WORD?

1. water fountain
2. at the zoo
3. in the bike rack
4. jogging path
5. trash can
6. bridle path
7. band shell
8. grill

B. ANALOGIES

1. sandbox
2. bridle path
3. duck pond
4. rest rooms
5. jogging path
6. tire swing

C. WHAT ARE THEY TALKING ABOUT?

1. jungle gym
2. duck pond
3. water fountain
4. seesaw
5. bench
6. rest rooms
7. zoo
8. statue

D. LISTENING: *WHAT ARE THEY TALKING ABOUT?*

Listen and circle the correct word.

1. Don't go so high! Be careful! You'll fall!
2. It's closed. We can't get in!
3. There are swings and a slide!
4. Let's go over there. There are tables and a grill.
5. The children really enjoy playing in it!
6. Have a drink! The water's cold!
7. Please throw this away for me.
8. Can we please ride on it?

Answers

1. jungle gym
2. rest room
3. playground
4. picnic area
5. sandbox
6. fountain
7. trash can
8. carousel

WORKBOOK PAGE 100

A. MATCHING: *WHAT DO THEY DO?*

1. c
2. d
3. a
4. b
5. f
6. h
7. e
8. g

B. WHICH WORD?

1. beach umbrella
2. sunglasses
3. kite
4. blanket
5. refreshment stand
6. beach ball
7. swimsuit
8. bucket
9. swimmer
10. waves

C. ANALOGIES

1. bathing cap
2. swimsuit
3. kite
4. lifeguard stand
5. raft
6. wave

D. LISTENING: *WHAT ARE THEY TALKING ABOUT?*

Listen and circle the correct word.

1. Would you like to sit down?
2. There's no air in it!
3. Put this on and your hair won't get wet.
4. Here. Use this to dry off.
5. Put this on. You won't get a sunburn.
6. Just a minute. I have to get my surfboard.
7. I'll put this down and we can sit on it.
8. Do you have one for me?

Answers

1. chair
2. raft
3. bathing cap
4. towel
5. sunscreen
6. surfer
7. blanket
8. life preserver

WORKBOOK PAGE 101

A. WHAT ARE THEY?

Things you throw:
darts
frisbee

Things you wear on your feet:
bowling shoes
jogging shoes
walking shoes

Things you wear on your hands:
handball glove
boxing gloves

B. MATCHING: *ASSOCIATIONS*

1. d
2. c
3. b
4. a
5. f
6. g
7. e

C. WHICH WORD?

1. stirrups
2. helmet
3. safety goggles
4. frisbee
5. weights
6. trampoline
7. stick
8. arrow
9. uniform
10. handball

D. ANALOGIES

1. paddle
2. golf club
3. roller skating
4. archery
5. skydiving
6. billiard balls

WORKBOOK PAGE 102

A. WHICH SPORTS?

1. baseball, softball, football, lacrosse, hockey
2. football
3. baseball, softball, football, lacrosse, soccer
4. hockey

B. CROSSWORD (see p. 152)

WORKBOOK PAGE 103

A. MATCHING: *ASSOCIATIONS*

1. e
2. g
3. a
4. d
5. h
6. c
7. b
8. f

B. WHICH WORD?

1. helmet
2. mask
3. stick
4. hoop
5. helmets
6. glove
7. hockey
8. uniforms

C. WHICH WORD DOESN'T BELONG?

1. shinguard (The others are worn on the head.)
2. bat (The others are items hit during the game.)
3. backboard (The others are used for hitting.)
4. shoulder pads (The others are worn on the hand.)
5. hockey (The others are played on a field or court, not on ice.)

D. LISTENING: *WHICH SPORT IS IT?*

Listen to the radio announcer and write the number next to the correct picture.

1. Nice pass! He's going toward the basket. He misses! He gets the rebound. It's in!!
2. The ball is hit into left field. The left fielder is running. He catches it. Oh! The ball falls out of his glove!
3. He's got the ball. But oh no! He drops the stick!
4. Good pass. He slams the puck! Goal!
5. It's a long pass! He caught it! He caught it! He's going for a touchdown!
6. He kicks. It's a goal!

Answers

| 2 | 5 | 3 |
| 4 | 1 | 6 |

WORKBOOK PAGE 104

A. WHICH SPORTS?

1. downhill skiing, cross-country skiing
2. ice skating, figure skating
3. snowmobiling
4. sledding, bobsledding, snowmobiling, tobogganing

B. MATCHING: *WHERE?*

1. c
2. d
3. a
4. e
5. b

C. WHICH WORD?

1. poles
2. skating
3. snowmobile
4. bobsledding
5. toboggan
6. Cross-country

D. MATCHING: *DEFINITIONS*

1. b
2. d
3. a
4. e
5. c

WORKBOOK PAGE 105

A. WHICH WORD?

1. surfboard
2. waterskiing
3. fishing
4. mask
5. fishing
6. sailing

B. MATCHING: *ASSOCIATIONS*

1. d
2. e
3. a
4. b
5. c

C. ANALOGIES

1. paddles
2. sailboard
3. wet suit
4. flippers
5. air tank
6. swimsuit

D. LISTENING: *WHAT ARE THEY DOING?*

Listen and write the number under the correct picture.

1. A. I brought my bathing suit and towel.
   B. Great! Let's go to the pool.
2. A. The ocean looks calm.
   B. I think the waves are big enough.
3. A. I got one!
   B. Look how big it is!
4. A. Here's the towrope.
   B. Thanks. I'm ready. Start the boat!
5. A. Can you show me how to use these?
   B. You don't know how to use paddles?
6. A. Is this your first time?
   B. Yes. It's fun to use the snorkel and flippers.

Answers

5	2	3
1	4	6

WORKBOOK PAGE 106

A. WHICH WORD?

1. bend
2. pass
3. Dribble
4. Dive
5. Shoot
6. run
7. stretch
8. Swing
9. Hit
10. Hop

B. ANALOGIES

1. shoot
2. throw
3. baseball
4. hands
5. hop
6. kneel

C. MATCHING: *ASSOCIATIONS*

1. e
2. d
3. b
4. c
5. a

D. LISTENING: *AEROBICS*

Listen and put the number under the correct picture.

1. Okay, everybody! I want you to stretch. Stretch those muscles. Stretch, stretch!
2. Now reach to the ceiling! As high as you can. Reach, reach!
3. Okay, now bend. Bend to the floor. . . bend, bend.
4. Now swing those arms. To the left, to the right. Swing, swing.
5. Okay. Now I want you to jump in place. Up and down, up and down. Jump, jump!
6. Now one foot at a time. Hop, left. Hop, right. Hop, hop.

Answers

5	2	3	1	6	4

WORKBOOK PAGE 107

A. WHAT'S THE WORD?

1. woodworking
2. photography
3. sewing
4. painting
5. astronomy
6. games
7. pottery
8. coin collecting

B. MATCHING: *ASSOCIATIONS*

1. c
2. e
3. a
4. d
5. b

C. ANALOGIES

1. coin album
2. knitting
3. knitting needle
4. bird watching
5. binoculars

D. WHAT ARE THEY TALKING ABOUT?

1. coin collecting
2. astronomy
3. sewing
4. bird watching
5. Scrabble

WORKBOOK PAGE 108

A. WHICH WORD?

1. audience
2. spotlight
3. lobby
4. balcony
5. company
6. tickets
7. chorus
8. baton

B. MATCHING

1. d
2. c
3. b
4. e
5. a

C. WHICH WORD DOESN'T BELONG?

1. usher (The others are places in a theater.)
2. billboard (The others are people.)
3. toeshoes (The others are people.)
4. ballerina (The others are groups of people, not individuals.)
5. ticket (The others are places in a theater.)
6. conductor (The others are dancers.)

D. WHO IS TALKING?

1. musician
2. usher
3. ballerina
4. actress
5. conductor

WORKBOOK PAGE 109

A. WHO LIKES WHAT?

1. music
2. play
3. TV programs
4. movies

B. LISTENING: *WHAT TYPE OF MUSIC IS IT?*

Listen to the music. Put the number next to the correct type of music.

1. rap music
2. country
3. jazz
4. classical
5. rock
6. gospel
7. reggae

Answers

4	1	2	5
6	3	7	

C. WHAT TYPE OF MOVIE IS IT?

1. cartoon
2. western
3. war
4. foreign
5. comedy

D. WHAT TYPE OF TV PROGRAM IS IT?

1. talk show
2. game show
3. children's show
4. news program
5. music video
6. sports show

WORKBOOK PAGE 110

A. WHICH WORD DOESN'T BELONG?

1. banjo (The others are keyboard instruments.)
2. accordion (The others are string instruments.)
3. trumpet (The others are woodwinds.)
4. clarinet (The others are string instruments.)
5. harmonica (The others are percussion instruments.)

B. CROSSWORD (see p. 152)

B. CROSSWORD (see p. 152)

C. LISTENING: *WHICH INSTRUMENT IS IT?*

1. harmonica
2. flute
3. banjo
4. tuba
5. harp
6. drum

Answers

4	6	2
1	5	3

WORKBOOK PAGE 111

A. WHAT'S THE WORD?
1. leaves
2. branch
3. grass
4. maple
5. tulips
6. palm

B. MATCHING: *ASSOCIATIONS*
1. b
2. d
3. a
4. e
5. c

C. ANALOGIES
1. trunk
2. flower
3. cactus
4. bulb
5. sunflower

D. CROSSWORD (see p. 153)

WORKBOOK PAGE 112

A. WHICH WORD?
1. river
2. forest
3. oil
4. valley
5. brook
6. hill
7. toxic waste
8. cliff

B. WHICH WORD DOESN'T BELONG?
1. desert (The others relate to water.)
2. rapids (The others relate to land.)
3. bay (The others are energy sources.)
4. ocean (The others relate to land.)
5. hill (The others relate to water.)
6. solar energy (The others relate to environmental problems.)
7. seashore (The others relate to areas of land with dense vegetation and trees.)

C. MATCHING: *WHAT'S THE PLACE?*
1. b
2. d
3. a
4. c
5. e

D. MATCHING: *ASSOCIATIONS*
1. d
2. e
3. c
4. b
5. a

WORKBOOK PAGE 113

A. WHICH WORD?
1. hay
2. garden
3. scarecrow
4. irrigation system
5. pitchfork
6. barnyard
7. sheep
8. barn

B. ANALOGIES
1. hen
2. horse
3. goat
4. chicken
5. farmer
6. piglet
7. calf

C. MATCHING: *ASSOCIATIONS*
1. e
2. a
3. b
4. f
5. c
6. h
7. d
8. g

D. LISTENING: *WHICH ANIMAL IS IT?*
Listen to the sounds of farm animals. Write the number of the sound on the correct line.
1. turkey
2. chick
3. cow
4. goat
5. horse
6. lamb
7. pig
8. rooster

Answers

5	8	1
6	7	4
2	3	

WORKBOOK PAGES 114-115

A. WHICH WORD?
1. kitten
2. stripes
3. gerbil
4. llama
5. pony
6. squirrel
7. monkeys
8. puppy

B. MATCHING: *WHICH ANIMAL IS IT?*
1. e
2. b
3. f
4. c
5. a
6. d
7. l
8. k
9. g
10. h
11. j
12. i

C. ANALOGIES
1. foal
2. rhinoceros
3. mouse
4. zebra
5. lion
6. beaver
7. dog
8. quills
9. gibbon
10. wolf

D. WHICH WORD DOESN'T BELONG?
1. raccoon (The others relate to horses.)
2. wolves (The others are rodents.)
3. buffalo (The others are parts that grow on certain animals.)
4. pouch (The others are external parts of animals.)
5. gorilla (The others are types of bears.)
6. mouse (The others are young animals.)
7. dog (The others are rodents.)

E. MATCHING: *WHAT DO THEY EAT?*
1. b
2. f
3. e
4. c
5. h
6. a
7. d
8. g

F. LISTENING: *WHAT ANIMAL IS IT?*
Listen and circle the correct word.
1. She wasn't happy to see a bat yesterday.
2. We heard a moose last night.
3. We saw a lion at the zoo last week.
4. What a big raccoon!
5. Look at that hyena!
6. Do you see the fawn?
7. Look at the donkey!
8. The anteater is a very interesting animal.
9. We went to the zoo and saw a koala bear.
10. Is that a leopard?

Answers
1. bat
2. moose
3. lion
4. raccoon
5. hyena
6. fawn
7. donkey
8. anteater
9. koala bear
10. leopard

G. MAKING COMPARISONS
1. bear
2. fox
3. donkey
4. pig
5. bull
6. cow
7. mouse
8. owl
9. bat
10. beaver

H. LISTENING: *WHICH ANIMAL IS IT?*

Listen to the sounds of animals and pets. Write the number of the sound on the correct line.

1. bear		6. hyena	
2. cat		7. lion	
3. donkey		8. mouse	
4. elephant		9. wolf	
5. gorilla		10. dog	

Answers

8	9	3	7	2
1	6	4	5	10

WORKBOOK PAGE 116

A. WHICH BIRD?

1. owl	5. penguin
2. hummingbird	6. peacock
3. pigeon	7. eagle
4. parrot	

B. WHICH INSECT?

1. spider	5. termite
2. firefly	6. tick
3. flea	7. bee
4. caterpillar	8. cricket

C. ANALOGIES

1. nest	4. web
2. bill	5. woodpecker
3. cockroach	6. feather

D. LISTENING: SOUNDS

Listen to the sounds of birds and insects. Write the number next to the correct word.

1. cricket	5. bee
2. crow	6. parrot
3. duck	7. seagull
4. owl	8. woodpecker

Answers

2	8	1	3
7	4	6	5

WORKBOOK PAGE 117

A. MATCHING: *ASSOCIATIONS*

1. b	4. f
2. c	5. a
3. e	6. d

B. ANALOGIES

1. snake	5. mussels
2. lizard	6. starfish
3. alligator	7. seal
4. claw	

C. WHICH WORD DOESN'T BELONG?

1. seal (The others are parts of fish.)
2. walrus (The others are snakes.)
3. whale (The others are shellfish.)
4. flounder (The others are sea animals.)
5. eel (The others are sea animals.)
6. crab (The others are large.)
7. iguana (The others live in water.)
8. tadpole (The others are parts of animals.)

WORKBOOK PAGE 118

A. WHICH HAS THE SAME MEANING?

1. b	4. c
2. d	5. a
3. e	

B. ANALOGIES

1. depth	5. ellipse
2. meter	6. diameter
3. square	7. wide
4. triangle	

C. MATCHING: *ABBREVIATIONS*

1. c	5. d
2. g	6. e
3. a	7. f
4. b	

D. WHAT DOES IT EQUAL?

1. mile
2. inch
3. yard
4. foot

WORKBOOK PAGE 119

A. DO YOU REMEMBER?

Mercury	Mars	Uranus
Venus	Jupiter	Neptune
Earth	Saturn	Pluto

B. MATCHING

1. d	4. e
2. c	5. b
3. a	

C. CROSSWORD: *PICTURES TO WORDS* (see p. 153)

WORKBOOK PAGE 7

B. CROSSWORD: *PICTURES AND WORDS*

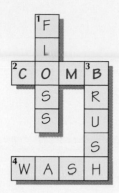

C. CROSSWORD: *WHAT DO WE DO?*

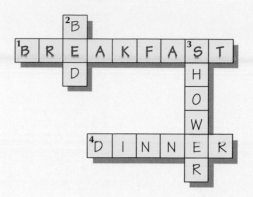

WORKBOOK PAGE 12

C. CROSSWORD

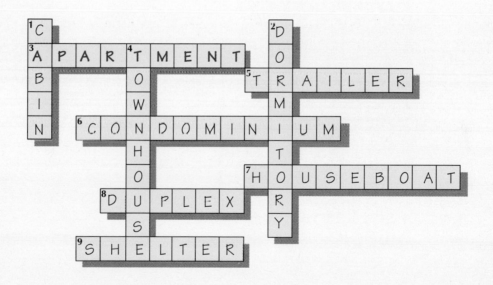

WORKBOOK PAGE 17

D. CROSSWORD

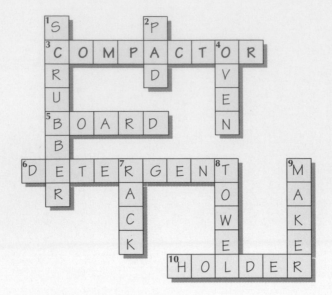

WORKBOOK PAGE 20

C. CROSSWORD: *PICTURES TO WORDS*

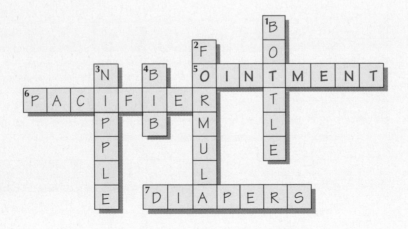

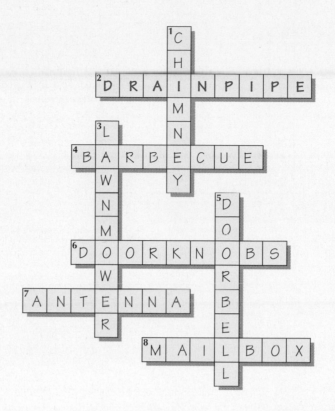

WORKBOOK PAGE 30

C. CROSSWORD: *NUMBERS TO WORDS*

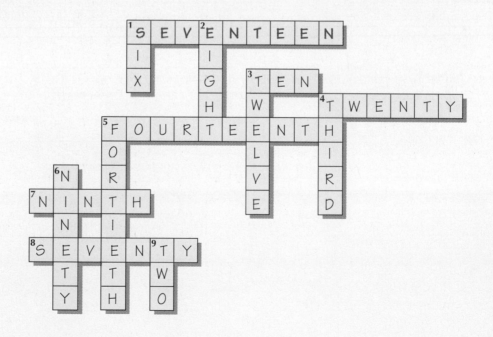

C. CROSSWORD: *PICTURES TO WORDS*

D. CROSSWORD: *OPPOSITES*

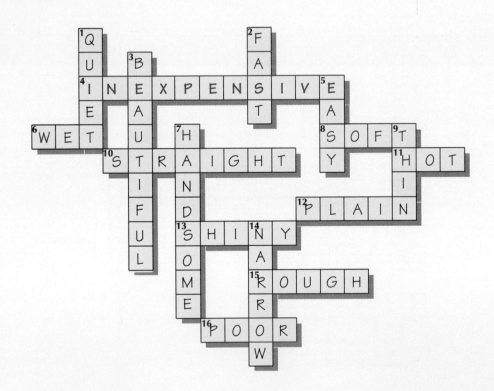

WORKBOOK PAGE 41

C. CROSSWORD: *PICTURES TO WORDS*

WORKBOOK PAGE 42

C. CROSSWORD: *PICTURES TO WORDS*

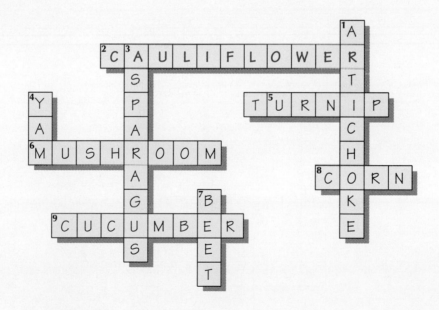

D. CROSSWORD: *PICTURES TO WORDS*

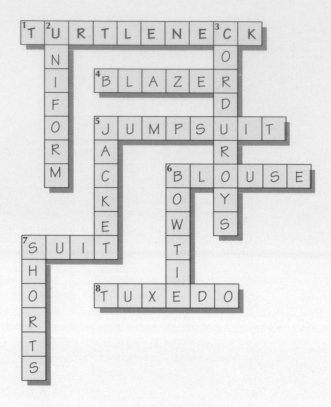

E. CROSSWORD

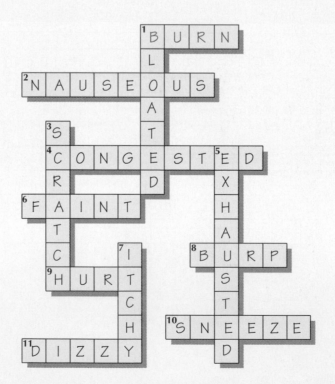

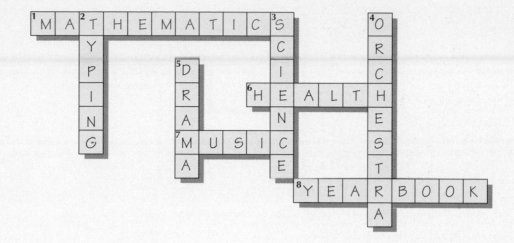

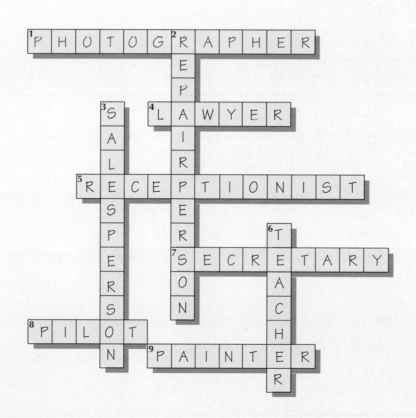

WORKBOOK PAGE 102

B. CROSSWORD

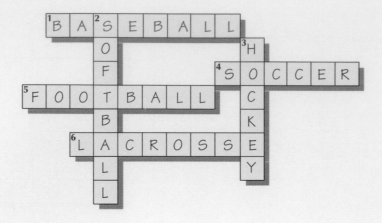

WORKBOOK PAGE 110

B. CROSSWORD

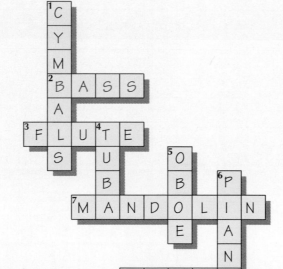

WORKBOOK PAGE 111

B. CROSSWORD

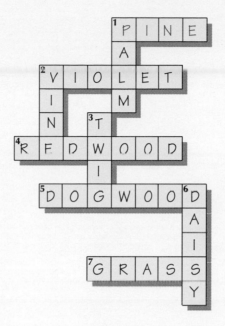

WORKBOOK PAGE 119

C. CROSSWORD: *PICTURES TO WORDS*

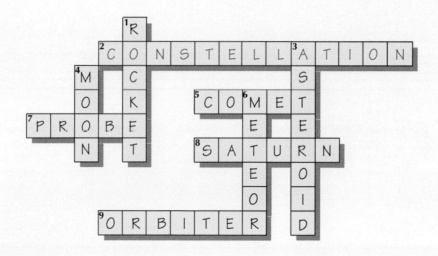